The Female

A step-by-step guide
to the adventure
that is starting your
own business!

By Charly Lester & Caroline Brealey

Copyright Charlotte-Cristina Lester & Caroline Oliver 2018

Ms Lester and Mrs Oliver assert the moral rights to be identified as the authors of this work.

All rights reserved. No part of this publication may be reproduced, stored in a retrieval system, or transmitted, in any form or by any means, electronic, mechanical, photocopying, recording or otherwise, without the prior permission of the publishers.

About the Authors

Charly Lester and Caroline Brealey are the founders of 'A League of Her Own' – an online membership club designed to encourage more women to start their own businesses. They are both successful entrepreneurs, and met through their work in the dating industry.

Charly Lester

The Founder of the UK, US and European Dating Awards, Charly has become one of the world's leading dating industry experts. Charly began her career in dating in 2013, when her dating blog 30 Dates went viral.

The blog led to Charly becoming The Guardian's first ever dating editor, and she was quickly head-hunted by Time Out Media Group, to work as their Global Head of Dating. Charly's dating advice has appeared in most British national newspapers, and she has appeared on BBC Newsnight, Crimewatch and Watchdog, representing the entire Dating Industry.

In 2015 she was selected as an expert advisor to Lord Sugar in the Final of The Apprentice. Charly is a regular guest on Radio 4's Woman's Hour. She teaches regular Masterclasses for The Guardian on a range of business subjects.

Charly is currently training for her first Ironman triathlon and the Marathon des Sables. She has two sausage dogs called Hugo and Dudley!

Caroline Brealey

Caroline never set out to be an 'entrepreneur'. Working in the voluntary sector with children with complex needs and their families, Caroline craved change and decided to turn an idea she'd had for a business into a reality.

Mutual Attraction, a now double-award winning matchmaking service launched in 2011. She has since gone on to launch the Matchmaker Academy, a training school for matchmakers which stemmed from her book 'How to Become a Matchmaker'.
Through the Academy, Caroline hosts regular training weekends, delivers 1:1 coaching and in 2016 she launched her first online training course for matchmakers.

In 2017 Caroline partnered with Charly to create 'A League of Her Own' - an online learning platform and members' community for budding female entrepreneurs to support them on their business journey.

Caroline loves nothing more than helping others, seeing businesses flourish and spending time with her family and sausage dog Lady!

Contents

Section 3 – Branding

Section 4 – Legitimising Your Business

Section 5 – Attracting Clients

Section 6 – Making Sales

Section 7 – Staying on Track

Section 1 – Introduction

"It wasn't that I decided to become an entrepreneur per se, it was more that I decided I was going to create something that I needed, and I knew women wanted, that did not exist at the time"

Bobbi Brown, Bobbi Brown Cosmetics

1. Welcome

Welcome and congratulations on taking your first step to your new life! Because that's what being a female founder is – it's far more than a career. It's a life choice!

If you want to experience the excitement of having an idea, putting it into action, and seeing it affect other people's lives – even in the smallest of ways - then we dedicate this book to you!

If you have a business idea, but don't know where to start, then you have picked the right book. We were both in your position once. We wanted to make the transition from working full-time for someone else, to working for ourselves. We knew what we wanted. We just weren't sure how to get from A to B. We'd never run our own companies before. In fact, we didn't even know other women who were business owners.

But you know what? We both did it, and we are going to show you how to do exactly the same thing. We'll also detail how to make a healthy profit from your new venture.

Here's what we can tell you about being business owners - it is incredibly rewarding, demanding and satisfying. Most people can only dream of working for themselves, but a growing number of people are taking the plunge, following their dream and making a career that fits their exact parameters. The very fact you are reading this book shows you have the ambition and drive to turn that dream into a reality.

Why this book?

When we were starting out, we didn't have peers we could ask questions to. We met each other a few years into our business journeys, and while we now know a whole host of other incredible women who run their own companies, when we were starting out, we felt alone. If you don't have role models, and can't see women like yourself starting their own businesses, it can be easy to just assume it's 'not for you'. Charly clearly remembers having the idea for the Dating Awards, but second-guessing herself because she was 'a woman, and women her age didn't run their own companies.' Charly is a confident woman, from an empowered, feminist upbringing, and with a law degree from Cambridge. If she was feeling some doubts, we know other women will feel those same doubts too. And the reality is that women DO run their own companies, and those women (and their companies) come in all shapes and sizes! We just all need to shout about it a bit more!

In this book, we will give you the support we wished we had when we were starting out. We will also include advice from other women who have started their own businesses. Some may be women you've heard of, others may be new to you. They all share one thing in common – they were where you are now, and they made a choice to pursue a dream and turn it into a reality.

How to use this book

This book will tell you step-by-step how to get your business from an idea to a reality. To make it easy for you to navigate we have started at the beginning of your journey, refining your idea and your brand, and will guide you through all aspects of launching your business, right up to when you have clients knocking down your door! Whilst this book outlines our experiences in the UK, this book is relevant anywhere else in the world. There may be some parts, particularly around registering your business, that differ but the concepts will still be the same.

The book is split into 7 sections and each is broken down into sections to make it easy to read and understand. We recommend reading from start to finish before launching your company. Once you've started your entrepreneurial journey, dip in and out of the book when you need to. Use it in the best way for you.

What's covered?

Anything and everything you need to know about starting and running a company. We will talk about refining your idea, branding, attracting clients and making sales. We will give you tips on making your money stretch and making your business stand out from the crowd. We won't just tell you WHAT to do - we will give guidance on HOW to do it.

There will be lots of real life examples from our own experience, things to avoid and things to consider. Expect lots of case studies, and tips and advice from successful female founders from a whole range of different businesses. There are thousands of women who have been there, done it… and survived!

Running your own business can be an incredible experience. Do it for the right reasons, be prepared to put in the effort, work hard and you can have a fun and rewarding profession.

Right let's get started!

2. Our Business Stories

Charly

So I basically fell into running an international company because of a joke, and the power of social media! It was the summer of 2013, and I had just 3 months left of my twenties. I got messed around by a guy I met online, and didn't want to spend the summer moping, so I set myself a challenge - to go on 30 blind dates before my 30th birthday. I posted a Facebook status, asking my friends to send me on the dates.

Within an hour, over 50 of my friends had commented or shared the post, offering up their friends, brothers, neighbours, and even husbands as dates for me! Five different people suggested I write a blog about the challenge, and thanks to my friends sharing stuff on social media, the first night I wrote the blog, over 2000 people read it. Over the summer of 2013, the blog '30 Dates' went viral. I had one of the most incredible summers of my life, and travelled to Madrid, New York and LA as part of the challenge. I went on some amazing (and awful!) dates! I dined in the dark, watched a circus sitting next to none other than Madonna, went to London Zoo, watched outdoor movies at Somerset House and had drinks in an underground bunker! And in the process I learned an awful lot about the realities of dating today.

As the blog grew in popularity, I began reviewing dating sites, apps, events and products. One of those events was a Guardian Soulmates singles events. Within 24 hours of me writing quite a critical review of the event, I was contacted by the Guardian, who asked me to work as a consultant for them. Two months later and I was given the role of Editor-in-Chief for the Guardian's Dating Blog. I took the job part-time, and continued working in banking. But six months later, I decided to trust my instincts, and see if I could work full-time in the dating space.

People had been emailing the blog from all over the world, asking me which dating site or app was the best. Rather than giving them my personal opinion, as a straight, female 30-something, I looked for a more democratic opinion. It was at that point that I realised there were no national industry awards for the dating industry. I set up the UK Dating Awards in April 2014, and the first event took place in November with 270 top execs attending.

The Awards solidified my position as one of the world's leading dating industry experts. With every set of awards, I sat on a panel of experts, judging apps, dating sites, matchmakers and dating experts. My position as CEO and Founder of the Awards led to regular mainstream media appearances. I became a regular on BBC Radio 4's Woman's Hour, and appeared on national news, and shows such as Crimewatch, Newsnight and Watchdog, representing the entire dating industry.

With every media appearance, and thanks to the success of the blog, my social media presence expanded, and at the end of 2014, I was approached by Time Out magazine. The media group wanted to create a dating site, and tie in the site with dating content around the world. In January 2015, the role 'Global Head of Dating' was created specifically for me, and I split my time between the singles scenes of London and New York for the next year.

In the summer of 2015, eHarmony approached me to write regular dating advice for their website. In January 2017 I became their UK Agony Aunt. That year I was an expert advisor to Lord Sugar in the final of the UK version of The Apprentice.

In 2016 I decided to take The Dating Awards abroad, running the first European Dating Awards in Amsterdam, and the first US Dating Awards in New York.

I am now recognised internationally as one of the world's leading dating industry experts. This was never something I imagined when I was young! I have a Law degree from Cambridge, and a Master's degree in Journalism! And yet the role fits me perfectly.

I met Caroline in 2014 when she entered (and won!) my first UK Dating Awards. We quickly became friends, and she joined my Judging Panel the following year. Over the years we've worked on a number of projects together, and we often discussed the issues we had when we'd first started out in business. We could still remember all the struggles and worries we'd had when we first came up with our business ideas, and we wanted to prevent other women being put off from starting their own businesses. We began working on A League of Her Own at the end of 2016 and launched the membership site and teaching platform to the public in October 2017.

Caroline

Some people love the idea of being an entrepreneur. They dream of ditching the 9-5 for something they're more passionate about. They visualise themselves working from quirky co-working spaces and being surrounded by the buzz of start-up businesses. I, on the other hand, was pretty oblivious to it all.

I had been working in the voluntary sector for several years when the idea for Mutual Attraction, my dating business, sprung into my head. I didn't have a business background, I had never done professional matchmaking before and I wasn't the most confident person.

But something about the idea wouldn't go away and I decided to go for it. I was petrified. I was worried people wouldn't take me seriously at 27, that I wouldn't make money and that I'd be left embarrassed if it didn't go to plan.

I'm not going to sugar coat it and say I never looked back. Because when my bank account was dwindling during that first year I did have a few 'what the heck have I done?' moments. But I pushed through them, and I am so glad I did!

It took a while, and some steep learning curves, but Mutual Attraction took off. We became busier, I began to employ a small number of staff and we won awards in the matchmaking field. I was even a finalist in the Great British Entrepreneur Awards, which was a great feeling.

A few years into running the business I decided to write a book about my journey, not knowing that this would lead to my second business, the Matchmaker Academy. I got such a great response from people who read the book and wanted to learn more about matchmaking that I decided to package up my skills and knowledge. At the Academy we train and support matchmakers through training weekends, 1:1 coaching and our online course. I'm so proud to have helped and supported matchmakers worldwide to fulfill their dreams of launching their own business.

Of course, it didn't stop there. Here's the thing about the 'entrepreneur bug', once you have it, it's very hard to shake it off!

Charly and I knew each other from the dating industry and both found starting our own businesses lonely, exhausting and more complicated than it should have been. We had both relied on trusty Google to provide us with answers to our questions! We talked about what a difference having a network of like-minded female entrepreneurs could make. Wouldn't it be great if you could get practical business training at an affordable price that wasn't filled with jargon and was actually relatable to us? So, A League of Her Own was born!

The best thing for me about being an entrepreneur? Being genuinely passionate about what I do and of course, being able to have the occasional day working in my pjs on the sofa!

3. Why only Female Entrepreneurs?

It's a question we get asked a lot.

So for a start … because we're both female and entrepreneurs! And so we have hands-on experience of being women and starting our own businesses. But it's more than that. Being a female entrepreneur is different to being a male entrepreneur in a number of ways.

Less than 5% of working women in the UK launch their own companies. And it has been proven that the main reason for that is fear. In a survey in 2017, 58% of working women cited a fear of failure as the reason they wouldn't launch their own company. The results of the same survey also found that only 37% of women felt confident they could source information and advice about starting their own companies.

This book is designed as a source of that information and advice. We also want to provide a whole host of alternative role models in A League of Her Own, because in our experience, there is a limited list of female founders who are presented as role models to women starting businesses, and the reality is that not every woman, or every business, fits the same mould.

Juggling motherhood and business is a challenge unique to female entrepreneurs. And an important one to discuss, because a huge proportion of women launch their first company while on maternity leave. In 2016 a survey suggested 1 in every 6 women who goes on maternity leave plans to start her own business. But not all those ideas become realities.

Investment is another area where start-up life is very different for male and female founders. A report in 2017 by the Entrepreneurs Network found that only 9% of funding into start-ups in the UK went to women-led businesses. Men are apparently 86% more likely to be venture capital-funded, and 56% more likely to secure angel investment.

The irony is that female founders have been proven to deliver better returns for investors. According to research by the Kauffman Foundation in the US, women-run technology companies achieve a 35% higher return on investment. And a recent study by the BI Norwegian Business School showed that women are better suited to leadership roles than men.

Don't worry – the situation isn't as grim as those stats may suggest. And you certainly shouldn't be put off by them. Because change is happening, and we ladies are right at the heart of it! Women now represent one in seven angel investors in the UK, a figure which has doubled in the last ten years. A report in 2016 from Founders4Schools showed that there were over 750 female-led companies in the UK with annual revenues of between £1m and £250m, growing at an average rate of 28% a year. Over a third of those companies were growing by more than 50%.

The world is waking up to the power and potential of female entrepreneurs, and as a result there are a whole host of initiatives and organisations out there to help and support you in your journey.

"The first day of running my own business full-time was terrifying. I kept wondering what I had been thinking quitting my day job. Everything got better from there."

Julie Falconer, A Lady in London

4. The different types of entrepreneur

Female business owners come in all shapes and sizes. Not just physically – though we know ladies starting their own businesses in their teens, and in their sixties! But also in terms of the businesses they run, and the way they run those businesses.

Running your own business does not have to mean quitting your day job, and committing full-time to your new line of work.

When Charly was starting her own business, she dipped her toe in the water. She began paid consultancy work for the Guardian, and only once she was sure she could pay her bills in this way, did she step away from her full-time banking role. We have a number of friends who have used this model at first – working on a 'side hustle' whilst still keeping their day job in order to pay the bills and build up some savings to invest in their business idea.

Your new business also doesn't have to be a brand new service or product. While some of you may well be reading this book with a great new idea for a food item or a game or a new app in mind, some of you may simply want to move away from full-time employment, and offer the services you already provide as an employee, as a consultant instead.

Sometimes people worry that their business idea isn't novel enough, but not every successful businesswoman we know created something new or novel. Many have launched companies in established industries, doing things which other companies were already doing – recruitment, catering, home-schooling. It's simply a question of understanding your offering and where it sits compared to your competition. What makes you stand out? What's your USP – your 'Unique Selling Point'?

Not all entrepreneurs are focused on one business, or one business idea. And the longer you work for yourself, the more strings you may find yourself adding to your bow. We are big advocates of spreading your eggs across multiple baskets, and having a variety of income streams. Some may be passive (where you do nothing, or very little), and others may require you to actively provide services or products in return for income. Caroline currently runs two different companies – her own matchmaking agency, and a matchmaker training school. The latter is to semi-passive, because she offers online learning courses, which are fully prepared and available online. Caroline also teaches live courses, however when someone buys an online course, the amount of time she has to devote to this customer is less than with her face-to-face students.

Charly owns a dating app, an Awards company, and also works as a paid consultant, teacher and writer.

The great part of being an entrepreneur is that you can shape your working week. You can choose where you dedicate your time, and what you do for a living. And if you're not enjoying something, you have the power to change it.

"A business is like a baby. Everyone offers you advice based on his or her experience. Take the advice you want, but do it your way. It's your baby."

Alice Walsh, Alice Made This.

5. Why work for yourself?

So why should you enter the uncertain, and variable world of the entrepreneur?

Both of us really enjoy our roles for a variety of reasons.

Flexibility and Freedom

There are few jobs that allow for the high level of flexibility that you have when you are your own boss. You will be able to work from home, fit work around other commitments and you can set your own hours either part or full time. This does mean you have to be a self-motivating person or else you can end up thinking 'just one more coffee before I start work'!

You can work in a way that suits you. For example Caroline works best in the morning, so she works 8-4pm, while Charly is a night owl, and often works until 2 or 3 in the morning! Caroline lives just outside of London, so she condenses all her meetings to one day of the week where possible. Meanwhile Charly never schedules meetings before 11am, because she knows she simply won't wake up in time! Charly's nighttime hours work particularly well when dealing with her American clients. As she works with a number of different corporate clients, she allocates specific days each week to specific clients. This allows her to be called into meetings or across the country at short notice.

Both Charly and Caroline live within easy reach of central London, because this is where most media appearances tend to happen, often at very short notice.

As an entrepreneur you can set your own routine based on what works well for you.

"I worked in big companies and had a burning desire to "do things my way." I found long processes held up projects and sometimes didn't succeed or even get finished. There were so many workplace traditions that I wanted to go away and start creating things on my own with no rules."

Emma Gannon, Ctrl Alt Delete

Career for Life

You are choosing this career for yourself. And you get to call the shots. You need to be passionate about what you're doing, because this isn't going to be an easy journey, but it has the potential to be a very rewarding one. And if you've chosen to do something you love, then hopefully this will be a career which keeps you far more invested than any other job you've ever had.

Fulfilling Career

Doing admin work at your local accountants might bring in the pay-cheques, but if it doesn't fill you with passion and make you want to get out of bed on a Monday morning then what's the point?

Do something you are truly passionate about. You're reading this book, which means the interest is there, now let us guide you through this amazing voyage.

"It's not all about the money. It's about enjoying what you do everyday."

Kate Jackson, TableCrowd

Excitement

Compared to our friends and peers, we genuinely have some of the most interesting, exciting and diverse careers. When you work for yourself, you choose which countries you work in, which events you go to, and what training you do. You choose who you do business with, where to focus your attention, and what your business does next. Yes it can be hard work, but it can be a really exciting adventure at the same time.

High Earning Potential

Obviously how much you make from your business idea depends what area you're doing business in, and how much time you put in. But, once you start working for yourself, there really is no limit when it comes to earning potential. You just need to make the right choices, and be prepared to put in the hard work. How much you earn will depend on your location, niche, choice of clients, and how much you decide to charge for your service or product.

However something which we have both realised, is that when you work for yourself, and every pound your company earns is a pound directly into your pocket, you'll be surprised how much extra effort you throw into things. When you run your own company, you know where every pound or dollar is being spent, and so you can create a highly profitable business model that you are fully in control of.

"Not On The High Street launched when my son Harry was just 3 months old, so I missed many of his milestones - first steps, first words. I spent so many sleepless nights, questioning my choices and convinced that he would be irrevocably damaged.

"In fact it turns out it is quite the opposite. At 9 years old he asked me if he could run a company one day, I told him that of course he could, his reply 'oh good, I thought only women could run companies.'"

Holly Tucker – NOTHS & Holly & Co.

6. The qualities needed to work for yourself

Do you have what it takes to be an entrepreneur?

While every business owner is different, in our experience, the most successful female founders all share several key qualities.

Self-Confidence

You don't have to be the loudest girl at the party, but you do need to believe in yourself. Because if you don't, you can't expect anyone else to. Yes, we all have doubts. And yes, we all have wobbles at times, but you need to be your own biggest cheerleader. Trust yourself and your judgment, and stick to your guns!

Passion

The vision for your business starts with you, so you need to understand it, and you need to care about it. This idea is going to monopolise your life. It will take up your evenings and weekends.

You will discuss it with your friends, your family, investors, the media... You need to be passionate about it! And if you're not? Then maybe you need to rethink your business idea.

Work Ethic

Unless you have a lot of start-up income, the reality of starting your own business is that you will be doing a lot of different things. As a female entrepreneur, there are times when you might feel like a general dogs body! Trust me, we've all been there – whether it's sweeping the floor at the end of an event, spending hours gluing things together, mastering Photoshop, or scheduling social media. You will become a Jack of all trades ... until you can afford to pay someone else to do them for you! So you need to be prepared to put in the hard graft.

"Get your life organized and take a vacation before you set your company "live", because your life will never be the same again!"

Amanda Bradford, The League.

Flexibility

Starting your own business is a learning curve. You may well be surprised where the journey takes you, and how quickly the goalposts can change. As a female entrepreneur, you need to be prepared to roll with the punches, and respond if an exciting change comes your way. Being proactive is a great skill, but you also need to be reactive and not overlook opportunities which may come your way. Many of the most exciting developments in Charly's entrepreneurial career were things she could have never foreseen.

"For me, the realization that you have to back yourself stands out. You can ask advice, but to be honest, other people don't always know – they don't have all the facts, and they aren't you. So trust your instinct and just go for things if you believe in them. Too many cooks really can spoil the broth, or stall you. "

Harriot Pleydell-Bouverie, Mallow & Marsh

Self-motivation

You have to be able to manage your time well, keep yourself motivated and full of positive energy, even when the going gets tough. Working for yourself, you are likely to experience peaks and troughs of work, and it's important to be able to push through the troughs. You have to be proactive, as clients won't just land in your lap. You are your own boss, and so you have to be able to recognise when you're slacking, and crank the gears where necessary.

"I think the scariest moments are when you go through a "quiet period" at the very beginning, when clients are on holiday or people are away, and you momentarily think you've made the wrong decision even though in the grand scheme of things it's all going very well."

Emma Gannon, Ctrl Alt Delete

Organisation

While we don't expect you to be hyper-organised (or even particularly tidy), if you are going to be running a business on your own, and particularly if it's starting as a 'side hustle', then you need to be organized with your time, and with your work. You will need to maximize the input of your time, and be quite ruthless at times about where you devote your energy. The more organized you can be from the start, the easier it will make your life, later down the line. If your career develops into a 'portfolio career' with different income from different sources, you will need to stay on top of invoices and make sure you know what money is owed to you, and by whom.

"Patience is key. Building relationships takes time and if they say no now, it doesn't mean no forever. I've had situations where people say no but then a year later, they come back and say yes."

Michelle Hua, Women of Wearables & Made With Glove

7. The steps to becoming an Entrepreneur

So you've read all about becoming a Female Entrepreneur and are ready to go for it. Great stuff!

There are 7 areas you need to cover when becoming a female founder but you know what the best news is? You have already done the first one!

The sections below give you an insight into what you need to consider, but don't panic, we are going to go into more detail and explain each one fully, this is just a taster for you of what is to come.

Is the career right for you?

Consider whether starting your own business is the right step for you by looking at the qualities and skills needed to start and run your own business. Are you prepared for the financial uncertainty (and excitement!) of working for yourself? Do you have to give up your full-time job? Or could you start your entrepreneurial career part-time / in your spare time? Do you have an idea which you are passionate enough to devote your spare time to? Do you believe in yourself even when others might not?

Starting a business isn't for the feint hearted … but that shouldn't put you off. There are hundreds of thousands of women all around the world who have started their own business. As Charly always says, whenever she's doubting her own abilities – look at your local high street! Every single shop was started by a business owner, whether it's a huge chain or a little corner shop. Every shop started because someone took the plunge and set up a business. And inside every shop, every product started with an idea. And every idea became a reality, because someone else took the plunge. You can take that plunge too!

The Ideas Phase

First you need to refine your business idea. Research your market to find out which services or products are already available and at what cost. Who will your competitors be? Are there gaps in the market? Who is your target audience? Get your creative juices flowing!

If you're not already an expert in your area of business, this is the stage in the process where we recommend geeking up on your chosen area of expertise. The better you understand your industry, the more likely you are to spot and exploit gaps in the market.

Branding

In this chapter we'll look at choosing the right name for your business. We'll discuss what to look for in a web domain, how to arrange hosting, and consider different ways to create a logo and build your business website. We'll also look at some of the more ideological aspects of branding.

Legitimising Your Business

In this section we'll talk you through registering your business, data protection, considering a trademark, are all the necessary things to ensure your business is run smoothly and professionally. We'll discuss business finances and different sources of investment for your company.

Attracting Clients

Once you're up and running, and have decided who your target clients are, how will you attract them? PR, advertising, social media and networking - which methods will you try?

Making Sales

Regardless what service or product you plan to sell, you need to sell it! Do you need a shop or an office? What are your options for meeting clients and how can you make a good first impression? In this chapter we'll also look at some tips for making high value sales, and advice on contracts and confidentiality agreements.

Staying on Track

Once your business is up and running, you will have new and different concerns. In this section we look at customer services, and dealing with complaints. We explore different ways to grow your business, innovative ideas for keeping your customers happy, and methods for keeping yourself on motivated.

Section 2 – The Ideas Phase

This is a section of business which really never stops. Whilst you obviously need an initial business idea to get things off the ground, as an entrepreneur, you will find yourself constantly having new ideas. (Just look at both of our careers!) The longer you stay in business, the more adventurous your ideas may become! Both of us keep notepads beside our beds, because the cliché really is true – you often have your best ideas just when you're drifting off to sleep! Charly also finds she thinks best about business stuff when she's exercising. She'll get out of the swimming pool or a yoga class and madly scribble down all the things she thought of while she was meant to be quiet!

8. The initial idea

Many of you will be reading this book with a clear business idea. Others may have several ideas. Some of you might just be reading this out of curiosity, or wanting to work for yourself but with no idea where to start. Everyone starts in a slightly different place.

In terms of the ideas, we believe they are always worth noting. Whether you do your research and then realise they're not viable, or you simply keep a list for future projects, keep notepads documenting your ideas process, or a list on your phone. Revisit the ideas from time to time – you never know when something might be more timely, or the opportunity might arise to pursue an idea you had earlier on.

If you're starting out with your first company, it can be helpful to start in an area which you know well, though that doesn't have to be the case. Charly had been working in and around the dating industry for about 9 months when she had her idea for the Dating Awards. The only large event she'd ever run before that was a University Ball. Caroline had never worked as a matchmaker or in recruitment, but she had worked with people before and could see a clear gap in the market.

If you haven't worked in that industry before, it's worth having a clear idea of the skills you can bring to the table, and things which might be transferable to your new areas of business. These may be things you later note in your business plan, and also chat about when you're at the bank, running over your plans with the bank manager.

Regardless of your experience, it's important that you are passionate about your idea. You need to believe in it, and in yourself, because if you don't, you can't expect others to! It doesn't have to be your favourite hobby, but you need to be interested enough in the topic to live it and breathe it for at least four or five years. Think about it – you're unlikely to apply for a job which doesn't inspire or interest you. When you're running your own business, it's like having a job 24/7! No, you're not necessarily working all the time. But it will often be on your mind even when you're not at work. Both of us often work evenings and weekends, and even if we're not working, we're thinking about ways we can expand our businesses, new products we can introduce, ways we can improve our service etc.

"I wish someone had told me how much my life work would be intertwined. It's difficult to never be able to "turn off", but I've gotten used to it over the years."

Julie Falconer, A Lady in London

Test the Water

Don't keep your idea to yourself. Talk to people about it. This is your first stage of market research. Practice your 'elevator pitch' explaining the idea in a few short sentences to friends and family. Does it make sense? What are their initial questions? Can you answer their questions? Not everyone will get it, and don't let that put you off. But by chatting to people about what you're planning to do, you'll get a good idea about the initial reservations, objections, and challenges. You will eventually need answers to these challenges. But if you are still passionate about the idea, in spite of those objections … well then you are ready for the next step!

"I came up with the idea and got so obsessed that I felt if I didn't pursue it someone else would. Although running my own business wasn't something I'd ever considered doing, funnily enough it naturally plays to my temperament. I'm incredibly head strong, determined and creative which gives me the tenacity and flair to give it anything a go and not give up when the going gets tough!"

Pip Murry, Pip and Nut

9. Researching the market

You wouldn't buy a house without first doing your research and the same applies to setting up a business. Before throwing yourself headfirst into your new life as an entrepreneur, you need to research the market.

In reality you will probably have already begun doing this without even realizing. Whether you were Googling competitors, or working out how much your product or services should cost, these are necessary steps in the ideas process.

Starting your research

The internet is a great place to start your research but don't forget other more traditional sources, such as the Yellow Pages, local magazines and newspapers.

Put aside a few hours one day, make yourself a strong coffee and grab a pen and paper.

Jot down all the words related to your product or service. A 'keyword' for Google is a 2-4 word phrase.

Now take a big gulp of that coffee, open a search engine up on your computer and type in your first keyword- for example 'date coaching'. Within seconds Google will provide you with links to hundreds of relevant pages. Click on the different websites and take a look around.

Here's a checklist of things you will want to look at:

If you're planning on offering a service ...

• Which competitors operate in your country and city?
• What services do your competitors offer?
• How do they deliver them?
• What packages do they offer?
• What is their price range?
• Do they operate in a niche area?
• How well-known are they?
• What's unique about what they offer?
• What do they do well and not so well?
• What are your initial thoughts when looking at their website?

If you're considering a product

• What similar products are available?
• Where can consumers buy them?
• How much do they cost?
• Where does your competitor manufacture them?

Don't worry about answering all these questions straight away.

In fact you might want to spend a few hours just taking a look around the different websites and come back to these questions another day.

It's important to try different keywords – they will produce different results. Not only will this give you access to more data, it will also make you aware of which keywords you will need to be using when you create your own website and marketing.

This is because each website has several keywords they focus
on. We'll come onto that later but that's why it is important to search all the different terms you can think of. Your searches are likely to bring up websites from all across the globe and this will give you an overview of the varying services or products out there. Once you have done this, if you are offering services specific to a certain area, you will want to refine your searches with geographic data – for example 'date coaching, Manchester'.

We recommend creating a spreadsheet to record all the information you gather. Caroline has one, which she still updates every few months to keep her up to date on what her fellow matchmakers are offering. It makes it easy to spot trends and also recognise gaps in the market.

Where possible, we also recommend testing out your competitors' services or products. Obviously don't spend lots of money on it, but if you can test out their services, or buy products relatively cheaply, it will help with your own research, so you know what standards and expectations you need to be meeting and exceeding.

What next?

You've collated all the information but what next? Your research should guide your thinking and the planning of your business. For example you may find there is no one offering a niche service in your country or area. This could be great news – but you need to make sure there is an audience for the service. The reason no one else is doing it may be because no one wants them to.

How viable is your business idea? Will there be enough people in need of your services or product? Is what you're offering unique and of interest to your target clients? To find this out you may need to carry out your own bit of detective work!

Identify your target clients, and ideally do some market research amongst them. If you have friends or acquaintances who fit the demographic of your target market, reach out to them and ask whether they, or any similar friends, would take a few moments to talk to you, or perhaps complete a questionnaire.

When Charly was starting her industry Awards, she spoke directly to her target clients – the dating app and website companies who would enter her Awards. Caroline needed to know that young Londoners would pay for matchmaking services, and so she approached her single friends with a questionnaire about using a matchmaker.

Don't panic if there are a lot people in your area offering the same service as you - that should mean there is a lot of demand! You will always have competitors and that applies to pretty much every industry and job in the world! What you need to consider is this; is there room for one more?

Top Tip

Don't be fazed about getting out there and talking to people.   Market research can be invaluable. We've found that people are flattered when we show a genuine interest and listen to their views.

10. Your target niche

You may decide your services or product are for everyone. However it may be more appropriate to offer your service to a particular demographic. Often by concentrating on a specific niche, you can better tailor your offering to your audience, understand your customers more, and also hone your marketing so it truly targets the right people.

Examples of niches include offering services specifically targeted to key groups including:

• Age niches e.g. over 50s or the under 40s
• Dietary niches – gluten free, vegan, sugar-free
• Tailored niches e.g. advice for people with disabilities

- Status niches e.g. high net-worth customers
- Geographical location niche e.g. based in New York
- B2B – only offering your services to businesses

Some of the best niches come about because business owners recognise a gap in the market where there is demand that is not being met. Be switched on and listen to what people are asking for. Also think about yourself as a customer. Is there something you need that no one else is offering? Some of the most successful food entrepreneurs have created products based on their own food allergies or intolerances. This links well to Brand Stories and Personal Branding, which are topics discussed elsewhere in this book.

"You can't compare yourself to anyone around you. Everyone has their own strengths and weaknesses and you will never really notice yours like you will someone else's. It's also true that your biggest strength is normally your biggest weakness. It took me years to figure that out and makes so much sense!"

Harriot Pleydell-Bouverie, Mallow & Marsh

Enjoy your area of business

Whichever area of business you choose, it's important that you
   a) understand it, and
   b) are passionate about it!

Because you are going to be thinking about it and talking about it A LOT! If you don't like working with high net-worth individuals then don't make it your niche! Let your interests and your instinct guide you …

11. Writing your Business Plan

A business plan describes all areas of your business. It outlines the business goals, attainable targets and how you are going to achieve them. Taking the time to develop a business plan now will be extremely beneficial for your business as it will flag up any potential problems, clarify your business idea and how you are going to achieve it. It is also a vital document if you plan on asking a bank for funding. It is a working document and will highlight lots of tasks for your 'To Do List'.

It might seem like a hard slog but there are a number of reasons why you should complete a business plan.

A business plan will:

• Determine whether your business has a good chance of making a solid profit
• Provide an estimate of your start-up costs and how much money you will need
• Highlight any areas to focus your efforts based on your research
• Anticipate potential problems so you can solve them before they become a real issue
• Be vital if you're talking to investors, and really useful for any meetings you need to have when you set up your business bank account.

The findings from your research will be of great use when completing your business plan.

True Story

Caroline has kept every copy of her business plan for Mutual Attraction. She was very optimistic in the beginning! The business plan was instrumental in getting her thinking and challenging her own ideas. This isn't always easy, if you've made up your mind to do something one way, but your research and business plan highlights flaws it can feel like a real set back. By questioning 'who, what, how and when' now, you will have much clearer insight into where you're heading. Spending time at this stage is invaluable. Ask someone to check it over afterwards. It can be easy to oversee things when we are so heavily involved.

Your business plan should highlight:

- What your business will do
- The services or product it will provide
- How customers will access your service or buy your products - in person or online?
- Your target customer
- Your approach to pricing e.g. how much will you charge?
- How will clients pay?
- How you plan on marketing and promoting your business

Writing a Business Plan

Writing a comprehensive business plan can be daunting but don't panic. Use the following headings to help you and check out the links at the end of the section, which will provide further information and guidance.

Executive Summary

The executive summary will be at the beginning of your business plan, but it's best to complete it when you have finished all other sections and have worked out the nuts and bolts of how your business will run. It will summarise the key points of your business plan.

Here you will outline your service or product and its advantages, your opportunity in the market, any experience you are bringing to the table, financial projections and any funding requirements.

The Business

Start by explaining the background to your business idea - for example how long have you been developing the idea and what led you to it. Highlight any work you have already carried out and any related experience you have. Don't forget that many of the skills you will have from other jobs and training will be transferable to your new role for example managerial experience, marketing, writing or public speaking.

Explain how your service or product will stand out from the others and how your clients will benefit from it. Now is the time to also look at any weaknesses or disadvantages in your business idea. Your business plan should be realistic. Think how your business will operate - for example will you be a sole trader? How will you register the business?

Top Tip

Forget the jargon and use plain English. Make your business plan clear and easy to read and understand.

Markets and Competitors

Who will be your target audience - do you have a specific niche? If so, how big is that niche and what does a typical client look like - think about age, sex, income, religion, location etc.

Who are your main competitors? Make a list of their advantages and disadvantages. Think about why people would choose to come to you instead. Getting this right now will enable you to market your services to the right people.

Sales and Marketing

This section is a biggie and you will need to answer the following:

- How will your service or product meet your clients' needs?
- How will you position yourself? For example, how much will you charge?
- How will you sell to potential clients? Via your website, face-to-face or through other means? How long do you predict it will take to sign up your first client?
- What does your first customer look like?
- How will you promote your service? Will you use advertising, PR, word of mouth?
- Examine your likely sales margins and costs. Where do you predict you will make profit?

Management

Are you going into business alone or with others? Outline who will be running the business and their responsibilities. If you are looking for funding you will really need to show your dedication and commitment to making your business a success.

Operations

Here you discuss where you will operate your business from and any equipment you need. Luckily most start-ups, particularly services, are easy to start with very few resources. It's easy to operate from home, and you will often need little more than a laptop and an internet connection to get started.

Think about all the tasks you will have to get done - will you need other staff members and if not how do you plan on completing all the tasks?

Financial Forecast

Your financial forecast translates what you have already said about your business into numbers.
This section will contain your:

- Realistic sales forecast. How many customers do you predict you will attain and by when?
- Cash flow forecast. How much money will be coming in and out of your business bank account and when?
- Profit and loss forecast. This will indicate how the business will move forward.

Financial Requirements

If you are planning on going to the bank to ask for financing you will need to outline how much you are looking for and prove that you will be able to pay it back. The work you did in the previous section will all feed into here.

Assessing the Risk

Consider a range of what-if scenarios - for example what if sales are lower than expected or much higher than forecasted? If you're offering a service, how will you manage if several clients join at once?

Helpful Resources

We recommend using a template to create your business plan. This will ensure you cover all areas and consider all factors. Free templates can be found at www.gov.uk/write-business-plan and www.bplans.co.uk/ For further reading we suggest 'How to Write a Business Plan' by Mike McKeever and 'Business Plans for Dummies' by Paul Tiffany and Steven D Peterson.

12. Skilling Up

Personal branding has become a big part of being an entrepreneur in 2018. Publicity and social media will often focus on the founder behind the product or service, and so we highly recommend becoming an expert in the field you're choosing to go into business in. Not only will this give you confidence to find gaps in the niche, it will also increase the likelihood of organic PR opportunities, and help you add depth to your brand marketing strategy.

There are wide range of ways you can become an expert in your chosen field. As we've already explained, passion is key to starting your own business, so hopefully you're already invested in and enthusiastic about your chosen subject. This should make it a lot easier for you to 'geek up' on the topic and truly immerse yourself in relevant news.

Are there any courses you can take related to your area of business? What books and magazines should you be reading? Can you showcase your knowledge on the subject on a blog? Could this blog even add content to your business website? These are all questions to consider.

Top Tip

Charly has always been a big advocate of Google Alerts. Set them up for keywords linked to your area of business. By keeping abreast of what's being written about your subject area of expertise, and starting conversations about those topics on social media, you can become a reliable source of information on your expert area. You can also identify trends quickly and be at the forefront of talking about them.

13. Co-Founders

"Having co-founders is like a marriage with 20 kids without sex. Chose your partners wisely!"

Stephanie Eltz, Doctorify

In the early stages it's worth deciding whether you plan to go into business alone, or with a co-founder. There are positives and negatives to both. Obviously working alone, you are likely to have more responsibility and potentially more work, especially at the start if you do not employ staff. But when you work alone you have full control of the business direction - all profits are yours, all business decisions are yours. As a co-founder, you will share the responsibilities and the choices. You must steer the company together, and you then split the profits.

Working with a co-founder can be a massive support and inspiration. When one of you is having a down day, the other one will spur you on. You may also find you slack less, because you are responsible to your co-founder. It may also make it easier for you to take maternity leave and holidays, particularly in the earlier stages of business.

With all that in mind, if you decide to work with a partner, it's worth ensuring that you are on the same page. To some degree running a business is like a marriage. You will go through good times and bad, together! You need to be able to communicate well, and to compromise when the situation requires it. Choose your co-founder wisely.

We had worked together on a number of projects before we decided to go into business together. We'd also worked with other people on projects and had seen first-hand what happens when things didn't work so well. We recognized that we had a similar approach to things, but equally had different skills in different areas. If you're choosing a co-founder, it can help to partner with someone who has complimentary skills. In the tech industry, for example, a tech-savvy founder will often partner with a co-founder who has marketing expertise. One thing that is really important is that you both have a passion in your company. If you don't, cracks are likely to form early.

14. Dealing with doubts

When it comes to business, we women tend to doubt ourselves a lot more than men. That's why so few of us, comparatively, start our own companies

You need to believe in yourself and your business idea. Because at the start, it is that belief which will sell the idea to others.

The thing to remember is that we all have down days. And sometimes we have down weeks, months, or even years! Business can be a rollercoaster at times – with highs and lows, and it's how you handle the lows that will make or break your business. So you need to be your own biggest cheerleader, and surround yourself with people who believe in you and your vision. There will always be doubters and naysayers – just shut out those voices, and don't let them affect what you're doing. Some people will never get it! Charly has been in business on her own for five years now, and still gets asked the same questions at family barbecues 'What are you doing these days?' 'What exactly do you do?' 'When are you going to get a real job?!' Not everyone is going to be your customer. Not everyone fits into your target market. As long as you, your team, and your audience understand what you do, then you're all good!

"Take risks and always be yourself. Whether it's landing that new job or finally starting your own business... stop talking about it and go after it. Think of how much money, time, and mental energy you invest in your education, your apartment, your wardrobe, your TV shows, reading, your friends, family.

"What if you invested 20-40% of that into your true passion? Have the confidence in yourself and other people will believe in you as well"

Amanda Bradford, The League

Outsourcing

You don't have to do everything yourself. And you are not failing by asking for help. In reality, no one is great at everything, and your time may well be better spent elsewhere, rather than taking hours trying to do something that doesn't fall into your skillset. Charly always the same logic that she does when it came to hiring a cleaner. Think about how much it would cost to pay someone else to do the task. Then think about how long it would take you, and how much you could be earning / how much value you could add to your company in that time. Often it's far more economical to ask for help. Especially these days when it's so easy to find freelancers willing to work by the hour or day.

For 'A League of Her Own' we use a whole range of freelancers – from our make-up artist, to our photographer, videographer, graphic designer and web designers. Often there are tasks we could do ourselves, but we know they would either take us far too long, or we wouldn't be able to do them to a high enough standard, so we ask for help. And for the League, we try to ensure that we are supporting other female entrepreneurs at the same time. All our freelancers are female!

Peer Mentors

Surrounding yourself with peer mentors can be a great approach. Entrepreneurs who are at the same stage as you in business, or who work in the same space as you. They will understand the everyday troubles you are facing. You can share your wins, and your challenges, and if they work in the same industry as you, you may be able to help each other with recommendations, pricing, suppliers, and trends.

We got to know each other first as unofficial peer mentors. We regularly met for drinks or dinner with two others who worked in the dating industry. None of us were competitors, and we would often direct media enquiries and customers to each other, collaborate on projects, or just chat on the good days and bad.

There are different places you can find peer mentors. If you don't have any friends at the same stage in business as you, why not check out our League – **www.leagueofher.com** - it's a club specifically designed for female founders and women with business ideas.

If you don't have a co-founder, a peer mentor can work well as an 'accountability partner'. Check in regularly with each other to make sure you are hitting your goals, and not letting your doubts hold you back. We will talk more about this towards the end of the book.

"Keep those around you, your inner circle of people who you trust, very close by. Business takes you on such an incredible journey, but it can also be incredibly lonely, it can make you question every decision and your intuition. Those people whose judgment and guidance you can trust 100% are invaluable in business and beyond."

Holly Tucker, Not On the High Street and Holly & Co

Mentors

Some businesswomen prefer to have a more senior mentor – whether in a formal arrangement, or informally. A mentor is someone a few steps ahead of you in business. Someone you can ask questions, and ideally meet up with on a regular basis to discuss your plans and challenges. Where possible, it can be helpful to find a mentor from a similar industry so they understand the challenges you are facing. Check out Section 7 for some useful links and more on Mentorship.

Section 3 - Branding

15. Choosing the right name

For many people who offer a service, their name becomes their brand. However it is important to understand, that if you decide to follow this route, then your name will be heavily tied to your chosen area of work.

While it is not always necessary, you may wish to work under a separate brand name. Particularly if you have a common name, have plans for growth, or if your name is already prominent on Google in other areas or industries.

Caroline – "A name is a powerful tool and should convey and reinforce the key elements of your business, for example 'Mutual Attraction' conveys the feeling two people have when they have 'chemistry' and often comes before love. That's what my clients want and that's why they're coming to us."

Choosing your name can be tricky and there are several things you should consider:

Top tips from the Experts

● Choose a familiar name that conjures up a nice feeling for your clients.
● Avoid anything too cheesy and make it appropriate for your target audience.
● Check if the name can be trademarked – we'll come onto this shortly.
● Consider what social media handles you might choose to accompany the business name. Are they available on all relevant platforms?
● Does it pass the 'loud bar' test? Can you easily tell someone the name? Can they spell it easily if they only hear it and don't see it written down?

"I was in the shower one day when all of a sudden it occurred to me that Three Little Birds was the one. It was a nod to Bob Marley, but I also liked the fact that in England "bird" could mean woman. I didn't think about it for long because as soon as the name came to me I knew it felt right."

April Jackson, Three Little Birds

Is your name already taken?

If you plan on being a Limited Company (we'll come onto this) you need to ensure there is no Company with the same name already operating, or your request to register that name with Companies House will be rejected. To see whether your suggested name is available you can use the free company search, which can be found here: www.companieshouse.gov.uk/about/miscellaneous/name Availability.shtml

NB – you don't have to work publicly under the Limited Company's name. You can work publicly under your name, but have a separate name for the company registered.

Keyword Planner

Google offers a service called Adwords. This is where you can pay to appear on a Google search. This will be covered in more depth during the chapter on marketing but you should be aware there is an option in this free program called 'keyword planner'. Type your suggested name in and you can see how many times people have been searching for that term both locally and worldwide both for your term and similar ones.

There are lots of free resources on how to make best use of the Google keyword planner.

NB - It is worth bearing in mind that Google has become increasingly aware that their tool is being used to do free SEO research, so they are continually tightening up the process and making it more difficult to find the Keyword Planner.

Pitfalls to avoid when choosing a company name

• Using strings of numbers or letters. People prefer words they understand and can relate to.
• Making your name location-specific. Whilst you might only be operating in your local city at the moment, if your empire grows, then the name will need to change.

• Making the name too long. It will be hard to remember and you'll have fun coming up with a Twitter account name!
• Picking a name where the web domain isn't available.

True Story

Caroline - "It actually took me about 2 months to come up with 'Mutual Attraction' which seems so obvious now. I just couldn't see the wood for the trees and by the end I had come up with hundreds of possible names, none of which seemed like 'the one'. Until I sat with a friend having drinks one day and he blurted out 'how about Mutual Attraction'. I liked it, I liked it a lot, but made the assumption that there was no way such an obvious term would still be available for me to buy as a web domain. Still there would be no harm trying. I checked online and HALLELUJAH! It was available and I could buy it for just a few pounds. I snapped it up and wiped the sweat off my forehead, I had a name and now the fun could begin!

If you're really stuck with coming up with a name you could always go to a
'Naming Consultant' – an expert in the field of selecting the perfect name for
your company. But you better have a spare £20,000 those as these guys
don't come cheap!

Top Tip

Brainstorm! Ask friends and family and jot down any words and names that spring to mind. One of them will 'click'.

You will need to have decided on a name for your business before you can register it.

16. Web Domains and Hosting

Previously we mentioned that you need to ensure the domain name is available for your new name. There's nothing worse than coming up with the perfect name only to find it's already been snapped up! A web domain is the address you type into your browser to visit a web page, for example http://www.amazon.com

To see if a web address is available for you to buy, go to a web domain search website such as www.heartinternet.co.uk or www.godaddy.com and type in the name of your proposed company. It will tell you whether the web address is available for you to purchase. If it's not, it means someone else owns it. It may become available for sale at a later date but in the meantime you need to find a different address. If the web domain you want isn't available the website will suggest some alternatives that are available. This could mean a slightly different name or a different ending such as .co.uk, .london, or .me

It's always preferable to get either .com or an individual country domain extension for example:

- United Kingdom: .co.uk
- Denmark .dk
- Spain.es

Other options such as .biz are available but shouldn't be your first choice as most people will automatically think your website address will be .com or your country's specific extension. If these are unavailable, we would strongly suggest considering using a different name.

On average expect to pay under £20 a year for a web name, although premium web names can be much higher. Premium names are the more sought after ones and are sold for hundreds, and sometimes thousands of pounds.

Hosting

As well as buying the web address you will also need to have web hosting. Think of web hosting as the 'middle man' you have to go through to get your website live and on the web for all to access and read.

Caroline went through 20i to buy both the Mutual Attraction web address and hosting. When the website was ready to go live she gave the details to her website designer, who uploaded it to the web host page and ta dah…it was working!

If you are opting to complete your own website and do it yourself, the web hosting company you choose will be able to guide you on how to do this.

Web domains and hosting can be purchased through www.20i.com for as little at £5 per month.

17. Logo

It's important to have the right image from day one. Your logo will represent your brand and your product or service. It will distinguish you from your competitors. A good logo can bring more clients to your door and the more clients, the happier the business!

Why is a logo important?

People remember logos better than names and they provide a visual representation of your company and/or your services offered. A logo will help you stand out from the crowd, and whatever industry you're planning on entering, it's important to set yourself apart from your competitors.

What makes for a good logo?

• Simplicity. Think of the most commonly recognised logos and all of them are simple in design - for example apple, McDonalds and Nike. Many are either a stylized letter, or a simplified image you know well – like the WWF panda.

• Versatility. Does it work as well on a postage stamp as on a billboard? Think big and small!

• Broad appeal. You may love a pink themed logo, but will it appeal to all your clients?

• Make it timeless. Will your logo still be relevant in 20 years?

• Appropriateness. For example, if you're a matchmaker then a black gothic logo is unlikely to make people think of love, relationships and happily skipping into the sunset! Make the logo relevant to the service you offer.

• Ensure it looks professional and reflects the quality of the service on offer. For example there are plenty of free logo makers on the web but if you are going to be charging £8,000 for your service will the logo reflect that of a professional and high-end service?

Where to get a logo

There are options available for all budgets:

• www.logomaker.com Creating your logo and putting it on your website is free but if you want to use it on other material such as business cards you will need to pay a small fee.

• www.designcrowd.com Post your brief and within just a few hours freelancers will be designing your logo for you, you pick the best, pay and you have a new logo!

Alternatively you can have your logo custom designed for you by a design
company. It's advisable to find out their costs upfront and how many revisions you will be entitled to. Whilst it can be a little more costly going down this route you will receive your logo in various formats and it should be designed to a high standard.

A word of warning

Be cautious when outsourcing the making of a logo that it is not copied from anywhere else. Ask the designer to confirm this to you in an email.

18. Other elements of branding

In this day and age, branding is of key importance to businesses. Why? Because it's become an integral part of consumer society. Branding affects the choices we make as consumers. We often have more than one available source for a product or service. Branding is the driving force which helps us to determine between the available sources. By tapping into our aspirations and desires, good branding can make a product or service seem indispensable. We simply must have it! Strong branding not only captures consumer attention, it captures their loyalty – producing brand fans who will return time and again to your business.

Branding makes your business identifiable and memorable. It helps you stand out, but also makes statements on your behalf about the cost of your products or services.

In addition to your brand name and logo, there are a wide variety of components which make up your brand. And that brand is an intangible concept – one perhaps best summed up as the way other people describe your company to other people, rather than how you describe it yourself.

Brand values

These are the core beliefs which underpin your company. While this may be something you've never considered, it's likely that you can create a list quite easily. These values will affect all areas of your business – from the colours you choose, to the layout of your website, to your pricing policy.

When Charly set up the Dating Awards, 'transparency' was a key value, because she had a competitor who used an online voting system which the public didn't find transparent. There were a number of complaints inside the industry about the winners of awards, and how they had been determined, and so Charly realised that transparency needed to be a key fundament of her business. Other values which had underpinned her initial idea were 'honesty', 'celebration' and 'impartiality'. Charly never wrote down her values, however transparency and honesty inspired her to include lengthy rules, and clear details about the judging process on her websites. Impartiality is underlined by the judging selection process and the disclosure each judge is required to complete. Celebration is highlighted by the images and colours used on the website. Burgundy and gold are colours which not only imply celebration, but also a judicial fairness.

It's worth having a think about your brand values – particularly when you are in the planning stages of your brand name, logo, strapline and the colours and fonts you use for your business.

Brand positioning

Where does your brand sit compared to your competitors'? Is it high end? Budget? Is it local, national or international? Who is your target market? Think about your ideal customer in detail. Are they male or female? What age are they? What is their disposable income?

What's your USP – your unique selling point? How will you stand out from your competition? These are important questions to ask yourself, right from the start. They are also likely to affect other areas of your branding …

Strapline / tagline

This is the sub-heading for your business. Take a look around at the brands you interact with. It's amazing how many have a strapline, and how many you know. Whether it's 'I'm lovin' it', or 'Just do it!', straplines are a great way to get across your brand promise – what you're offering your customers.

A strapline is also something which you can change. So if your brand stands the tests of time, and you start to feel like your branding is less relevant, you can modernize by updating the strapline.

Style guide

These days, almost every brand will have a website, which is why, even if you don't use packaging, you are likely to need to make decisions about the colours, fonts, and overall tone which represent your company. Think about your values. Think about the pricing messages you are trying to convey. Who are your target audience? Look at other brands – bright green is often used for budget brands and products. Burgundy or gold convey a sense of luxury. Spend some time choosing colours and fonts which work well with your logo – often the fonts will be the ones you use in your logo. Finding a style you are happy with from the start will save you time later on.

We have a style guide template inside the League's Branding Module.

Brand story

In this day and age, your 'brand story' is an important part of your brand. This is one of the reasons why it can help to start a company in an area where you have some background.

People like to understand the story behind a company – particularly when it comes to PR about your brand. What inspired you to start? What problem are you trying to solve? Think carefully about the story behind your brand. It will come up time and again! You might even want to share it on your website.

"I believe a successful brand embodies an authentic business story. The great thing about business storytelling is that it has nothing to do with the numbers and everything to do with authenticity. For a brand to feel authentic and accessible you need to have a strong story behind it."

Lucy Chamberlain, C&C Search

19. Website

Once you've got branding sorted, creating your webpage will be high on your 'To Do' list. After all not many people will part with their hard-earned cash without first checking the internet. It's rare these days that a company won't have at least a basic website. Remember that first impressions of your company will often be made off the back of your web presence, so even if you have a single page website, do ensure it's one you're happy and proud of.

You have three options when creating a website
1) hire a website design company
2) get a freelancer, or
3) do it yourself.

When Caroline set up as a matchmaker she had no idea where to start, and the idea of doing it scared her half to death! As a result, she went to a design company who created both the logo and the website. This is the most expensive option, and in hindsight Caroline realised she needn't have spent anywhere near as much as she did. While she was happy with the end product, she realised she could have saved a considerable amount doing some things herself. (She also ended up changing the logo and the website five years later!)

By contrast, Charly designed her logo herself, using images from Shutterstock, and Gimp – a cheap version of PhotoShop. She used a freelancer to build her website, and then together they developed the logo and branding over the coming months and years. Every year it became a slightly more sophisticated version of the original image.

Before we go any further, we recommend you search your competitors, not just locally but all over the World. Grab a pen and paper and write down your first thoughts and impressions for each website before taking 10 minutes on each page making notes on the elements of the design you like. Perhaps it's the video describing the service, the banner or the colour theme. Make a list of what you like and what you don't like (sometimes the latter is easier!). This will give you a good starting point for creating your own site.

Next think about your niche and your target audience.

Caroline's company Mutual Attraction targets professionals. As professionals are used to seeing high quality and well-designed websites, an unprofessional, bog-standard template wasn't going to cut it. If your niche is working with Afro Caribbean clients ensure your website reflects this in its pictures. If your niche is working with high net-worth individuals and your fees are high, then a quickly thrown together, unprofessional-looking website isn't going to portray the right image.

Caroline's first idea for her website was girly beyond belief - pastel pink with a French patisserie look. It looked awesome, if she'd been selling poodle accessories! Asking friends and family for an objective view highlighted that the website looked more like a shop and that men would run a mile. Back to the drawing board it was!

Always keep in mind your target audience. You're not the one who's going to be looking at the website thinking 'shall I enquire'. It will be your target audience, so make sure it meets their needs above yours. Remember that whilst you may just want to think about the actual day-to-day business, without these things in place you will have no clients to do business with. It's important to get it right.

What should be on your website?

KISS – keep it simple stupid!

We're not calling you stupid (promise!) but the keeping it simple rule hits the nail on the head. What information do potential clients need to know? Keep it simple and cut the waffle. Most business websites need only be a few pages long. Any more and your potential client will get bored searching for information.

Services / Product

What is someone getting out of becoming your client? What are you going to deliver and by when? Why should they choose your service over others? Be clear and concise, your future clients will appreciate it. Some people may be new to the services you offer, so don't make them guess what you do, tell them.

If you are selling a product, make sure you have good quality photos, which clearly show your product.

Pricing

Not everyone includes pricing on their websites, however in our experience the easier you make it for your clients to find out information, the quicker they are likely to convert.

Photos

It is a good idea to use a mixture of real photos and stock photos. Stock photos are professional images you can buy to use on your website and can be purchased from websites such as www.istockphoto.com/ and www.shutterstock.com/

Whilst real-life or bespoke photographs make the website more 'real' they can also be difficult to obtain, particularly as you must have consent from the people in the photograph. If you are offering a service, it can be hard to convince real customers to appear in your photographs. Stock photos are much more marketing friendly, but can be a bit cheesy so choose wisely and avoid going for the same ones used by your competitors.

Testimonials

Caroline added a testimonial page to her website about a year after launching – once she actually had some testimonials to shout about! Although it's not always possible due to privacy, she always tries to have a photo of the happy couple.

In some industries real-life images are worth a thousand words. If you're just starting out there are ways to still get testimonials. Don't tell any fibs but get creative! If you do use photographs – always make sure you have permission to use the photos, and that they are of the person who has given the testimonial. Honesty and transparency need to underpin your business and your website.

We try to update our testimonials on the League of Her Own website at least every couple of months. And if someone sends us a lovely thank you email, then we ask if they wouldn't mind us publishing it as a testimonial. Most people are more than happy to support you if they had a good experience.

Testimonials can also be really useful later on when you start entering business awards.

Keep it fresh

This sounds simple but can be harder than it sounds! You are likely to tweak the content of your webpage quite regularly, but it's unlikely you will be adding the significant amounts of new material which is needed to keep your website fresh and to keep Google thinking your website is awesome!

The best way to do this is to create a blog. Not only is it a great way to keep your site constantly updated, but it's also a great way to showcase your expertise. A good blog can not only bring in new potential clients, but it can also gets your name out there when the post is shared. It will also help massively with our next area …

SEO

SEO stands for search engine optimization. In a nutshell it's the process affecting the visibility of your webpage in free search results on search engines. If you Google the service or product you're offering, and your area, you want your website to be coming up high on the results list. If your website is on page 7, it's unlikely people will click through for that long to find it.

SEO is important if your webpage is going to appear high in the search results organically (unpaid). There is a wealth of information available online and there are also SEO specialists who can advise you although these naturally come with a fee.

Having a good SEO rank is important and it is something you will be constantly developing but to get you started and heading in the right direction here are a few things you can do from day one:

Content is King

Regularly add new, unique and interesting content to your website. The key here is to make it relevant. If you write a blog post and just pack it full of buzzwords for Google, people will see right through it and won't hang around for long. That's not the impression you want to make, so make the content relevant and informative.

Top Tip

Don't forget to add social media sharing buttons so people can share your content. Just don't add too many, otherwise people won't bother sharing because they have too many choices. Research has shown that just 3 or 4 options works best. We suggest Facebook, LinkedIn, Twitter and email.

Internal Linking

Remember that great blog post you wrote a few months back? People who are reading your new blog post might also be interested in reading your old post. Link to it in the post so people can simply click through to it. Do this regularly and develop a 'linking mindset'. Internal linking can considerably contribute to your SEO and it's simple and quick to do.

Citations

A citation is the official term for when someone mentions you or your business on their website. It could be a link to your webpage, your business address listing on an online directory or a comment you have left on someone's blog under your business name.

Getting your name out there as much as possible is good, because Google and other search engines pick up on citations. In theory the more citations the better your SEO ranking and the higher you appear in search engines. Most service providers operate in a particular geographical area and citations are especially important because search engines use them to help determine where you are operating. Luckily for us there is lots of helpful guidance already out there on how to create and build up citations, and a good place to start is by checking out this extensive list www.localstampede.com/citation-building-strategies-list/

A good example of a citation is Google's free 'Places for Business' feature. Simply register key details such as your business address, phone number and working hours and once Google has verified the details by sending you a postcard to your address with a code, your business details will be featured on Google.

Visit http://www.google.co.uk/business/placesforbusiness/

Some recommended reading to develop your knowledge of SEO:

http://moz.com/beginners-guide-to-seo

http://www.youtube.com/watch?v=hF515-0Tduk
http://www.seomark.co.uk/

How to get your website created

So now you have an idea of what your new webpage is going to look like and what content you're going to put on it, it's time to consider how and who is going to produce it.

Design Company

A professional design company will tailor-make your website based on your brief. They will take care of all aspects of the design and should ensure that it's user-friendly, providing you with basic training on how to use the website to update your content.

One of the advantages of using a design company is the reliability. You will often have a contract specifying the end date of the project and if they are a reputable company they will show you examples of their previous work. It can be expensive and you should be prepared to pay a few thousand pounds for a custom-made website, however it can be worth it if you have very clear ideas on how the website will look. Using a specialist service is also beneficial if you want 'extras' such as a private members' area.

Go Freelance

There are thousands of freelance website designers around looking for work.

Sites such as http://www.peopleperhour.com are a great place to start. They allow you to either search through freelancers and approach them about your project or place the job for free and freelancers will 'bid' on your project outlining what they can deliver, by when and at what cost. Always ensure you check out any references first and see examples of previous work. You will find experienced designers and those just starting out and each will range in price significantly so there will be someone available whatever the project.

DIY

If you are creative, good at computers and have time to invest in developing a website, then why not give it a shot yourself. With hundreds of free Wordpress themes available it's never been easier to set up your own website. Caroline is practically allergic to computers and even she managed to whizz up her own professional page: www.carolinebrealey.co.uk. While it may not win any awards for creative design, it does the job!

Similarly, Charly uses a simple Wordpress template for her website **www.charlylester.com**. Wordpress themes can be found for free or for a small charge. Simply do a Google search and you will find endless designs from the simple to the complex and from the snazzy to the dull. Many websites are now operated by Wordpress including websites for big names such as Katy Perry, StyleWatch and Jay-Z. If it's good enough for Katy, it's good enough for us!

However if you aren't very tech savvy it may be worth considering a different option.

Top Tip

Consider placing an ad at your local University. There are hundreds of web design and computing students out there looking for ways to develop their portfolio and earn a bit of extra money at the same time!

"Time is often more valuable than money so if you can outsource some tasks that you don't like/aren't good it – do it!"

Hannah Witton, YouTuber and Author

One last word on websites

Websites should never just be static. Keep going back to your webpage and updating bits. If your prices change, you need to update them immediately. If you put date-specific information on - for example 'we will be closed between Christmas and New Year' - make sure it's taken down at the appropriate time. Any little thing can ruin your brand and reputation, so make updating your website a part of your schedule and you'll reap the rewards.

Section 4 – Legitimising Your Business

20. Registering Your Business

You've done your homework, you've researched the market until you're blue in the face, you have your name and now you're ready to take the step to start your business.

You're excited, a little nervous and ready to get cracking! Before you can start working with clients there are a few important hoops you have to jump through first, including registering your business.

"I was excited when my first company's certificate of incorporation arrived in the post! With each company I've launched, the first sale is always a very proud moment. It is the point that someone wants to buy the thing you have created from scratch."
Kate Jackson, TableCrowd

Sole Trader or Limited Company?

Whilst not the only options, most small businesses operate as a Sole Trader or a Limited Company. All of our businesses are Limited Companies.

Sole Trader

A sole trader runs their own business as an individual. You can keep all your business' profits after you've paid tax on them. A sole trader is personally responsible for the business including any losses the business makes, keeping records of your business' sales and spending, and for paying bills related to your business. You will be responsible but you can still take on employees.

To set up your business as a sole trader you must register for Self-Assessment with HM Revenue & Customs (HMRC). You can do this here: www.gov.uk/register-for-self-assessment

Limited Company

A limited company is an organisation that you can set up to run your business. Unlike a sole trader, the company is responsible in its own right for everything it does and the company's finances are separate to your personal finances.

Any profit the company makes is owned by the company, after it pays Corporation Tax. The company can then share its profits amongst its shareholders, you can have several shareholders or it could be just yourself.

There are different types of Limited Companies and there are many legal responsibilities involved with being a Director and running a limited company. Further information can be found by visiting:

https://www.gov.uk/business-legal-structures/limited-company

You will need to register, or in professional terms 'incorporate', your new company with Companies House before you can begin operating. This is a relatively straightforward process and can be done online at http://www.companieshouse.gov.uk. It currently costs £15 (if completed online). Once you have submitted your form you may need to wait a few weeks while your application is processed. Once your application has been accepted you will receive a 'Certificate of Incorporation'. This means your Company is now legally registered and you can get started growing your new business.

Whilst we can only cover the basics here, using the following resources will provide you with more in depth information:

The Small Business Start-up Kit; A step by step Legal Guide by Pakroo J.D., Peri (2012) available for purchase from Amazon.

www.sole-trader-or-limited-company.co.uk/

21. Trademarks

Trademarking your company name is not a necessity but it is advisable as it provides a high level of protection for your business. For example without a trade mark someone in Scotland could set up a matchmaking service called Mutual Attraction. This might not seem like a problem because Caroline's company is London-based at present but what about if she chooses to expand nationwide? It will also cause confusion for clients when looking online, they are likely to find information on both Mutual Attraction in Scotland and London – confusing! By having a trademark you can protect your business identity, your brand and your name. You've worked hard to build it up so don't just give it away.

There are lots of companies out there who will happily help you get your trademark but they come at a price. The best thing to do is apply online directly with the Intellectual Property Office at www.ipo.gov.uk/ Expect to pay approximately £200, although if you apply online you will receive a discount so ditch the paper! Just be aware – trademarks are local to one country, or you can apply for a European Union trademark. You will need to register in every country or territory you wish to be covered in.

22. Data Protection

Depending on the service or product you are offering, you will be gathering different personal information about your clients.

If you are storing personal data about a person you will need to abide by the Data Protection Act 1998 which requires you to register with the Information Commissioners Office (ICO). This sounds far scarier than it really is. It's actually a relatively straightforward process and once you have registered you can renew automatically each year.

At present it costs £35 and you can complete your application form online at www.ico.org.uk

Until you have registered with the ICO you should not be storing personal information and it can take several weeks for your registration to come through so we recommend doing this shortly after registering your business, depending on the services you're offering and the data you're collecting.

From May 2018 the GDPR (General Data Protection Regulation) also applies. A key facet of the regulation is that you need explicit opt-in consent to include someone's email address on a mailing list.

23. Back-up System

If details of your business are stored on a computer, make sure you have a back-up system in place from day one. Think of the worst case scenario - your laptop gets stolen or you leave it on the train. It happens. Make sure you back up your records regularly, and consider cloud storage.

You may want to consider backup.comodo.com/

Virus Protection

We've all been there before. Opened an attachment on an email, clicked onto the wrong website or just turned our computer on one day only for it have been taken over by a bad ass virus that shows no sign of budging. Make sure your anti-virus software is up to date; you can get free software from various websites including http://www.avast.com/index or http://free.avg.com/us-en/homepage

24. Initial Investment

To set up your business you will need some money. No matter how money-cautious you are, there are still some costs that you will have to pay.

The amount of those overheads will vary greatly depending on the nature of your company. If you're creating a product, the production stage will require investment so you can create stock. You may have to pay for materials, storage, packaging. Even if you are starting a service-based business, there may be costs you can't avoid – such as setting up a website and paying for business insurance.

Consider your options for sourcing the initial capital.

Savings

If you can, the best way to finance your new business is by yourself. What we hope we are showing you throughout this book is that there are ways to set up your business without it costing the earth. What can you afford to put away each month towards your new career?

Try breaking it down into steps over a 12-month plan. Month 1 you pay for incorporating the company (£15) months 2 and 3 you pay a freelancer to set up a simple website (£250), month 4 you register for Data Protection (£35) and so on. With some forward planning you can set up your business without even missing the money!

Bank Loan

Finding a bank willing to lend to a small business these days is a tough task. But it's certainly an avenue worth pursuing if you are unable to get finance from elsewhere. The best thing to do here is to look on each banks webpage regarding their loans for small businesses. Contact them direct by phone and chat over your business plan with an adviser who will be able to recommend whether you should see a business manager to discuss it further. If you are going to ask a bank to provide a loan you will need a seriously kickass business plan so make sure you invest time and energy into it.

Grant

It can be difficult to get a grant but not impossible. A grant is non-repayable and often given by government. It is always worth checking out what grants are available, and whether you meet the criteria for applying. Try searching for local grants online or check out the Small Business website which outlines all government grants currently available:

www.smallbusiness.co.uk/financing-a-business/government-grants/

www.startups.co.uk/grants-for-starting-a-business.html

Make use of family and friends

The idea here is that someone does something for you and you give them something in return. For example if you're not very clued up on social media but know your cousin is a whizz. Why not ask them for some help? In return you can make them that amazing chocolate cake you know they love. Utilize those around you, it's amazing what friends and family will do with the promise of a glass or two of wine at the end! Social media can be a great way to reach out to friends for help with specific tasks.

A number of Charly's friends still volunteer at her Awards ceremonies because they are so much fun, and the team of volunteers has travelled around the world with her. You'll be amazed how much help you can get when you ask people – and social media is a great place to approach friends and family. One of the realities of running a business is that we are still in the minority and our friends with more conventional lives are excited by what we do and often want to get involved!

Crowd-funding

An increasingly popular method for modern start-ups to get early finance is crowd-funding. You can obviously do this informally, by reaching out to friends and family and asking them to invest in your business idea – with either equity or some form of other reward in return - or you can arrange crowd-funding more formally on a crowd-funding website. These sites include Kickstarter, Indiegogo and RocketHub. On these sites, strangers can pledge money to your start-up in return for all kinds of rewards – anything from a hug, to a bag of popcorn, to themed stickers or badges or clothing. You decide what rewards you send to your supporters. The key part is – they don't get equity in your company. Essentially they are donating money to your cause, and getting a token gift as a thank you for the support.

Investment

More conventional investment involves giving investors a share of your company in return for their financial investment. The share of the company is known as 'equity'. You are likely to have to provide detailed financial forecasts for your business, showing how much you expect the business to be worth in 5 years time. These forecasts will be used to work out how much of your business the investor should receive in return for their money.

Investment can happen at any point in your business journey, it's not exclusive to starting up. Many companies will go through multiple rounds of funding, bringing in more investors at points when the company needs more cash to grow. However, when investment occurs at start-up stage, it is known as 'venture capital'.

Most start-ups which require venture capital will either source it from high net-worth individuals, known as 'angel investors' or from specialist venture capital firms. Venture capital firms will specialise in identifying innovative and promising start-ups to invest in. The good news for us, is that there are an increasing number of VC firms keen to invest in female entrepreneurs – including the London-based Allbright Foundation.

Be aware, investors will look carefully at your background and track record. Without an existing company to evaluate, they will pick apart your business idea, and assess your ability to turn it into a profitable business.

Before sourcing and accepting external investment, we'd suggest you think very carefully about whether you need the money. Equity in your company is a valuable thing, and not something to be thrown about. Both of us own 100% of our companies. We started our businesses with minimal costs, and designed business models which allowed us to become profitable quickly. As a result, we were able to maintain full ownership of our companies, which was important to us both, because it not only means we reap all the profits from the businesses, it also meant we retained full control of the businesses, and didn't have to answer to anyone else about the business decisions which we have made along the way.

25. Business Banking

Setting up a business account

You will need a business account so that clients can pay you.

Before you decide on a bank, it's worth researching what they offer small businesses, and whether they have any special deals available. Some banks will offer specific services for small businesses, others will offer free services for the first 12 or 18 months. Expect to pay a monthly fee of roughly £5 for your business bank account. If you need foreign currency accounts, or the ability to make international payments, these services will raise your monthly fees.

When you set up a business bank account, you will be required to set up a meeting at the bank. Before the meeting you will need to have registered as a sole trader or a limited company, and you will need to bring proof of your registration to the meeting. We recommend bringing a copy of your business plan to the meeting too. When the bank provides you with an account, they may also be offering you overdraft and credit facilities – so before they commit to lending your business money, they will want to assess the viability of your business. Expect to have to explain how your company will make money, and projected annual income and outgoings.

Case Study

The first time Charly opened a business bank account, she didn't realise she would have to explain her business idea to the bank manager. Because she didn't need an overdraft or a credit card, she thought it would be as simple as filling in a form and opening the account, however in the end she had to spend over an hour, explaining how a corporate awards company makes money. 'But who will pay to enter?' the bank manager asked. 'And have you done any research to ensure the company is viable?' Luckily Charly had worked in the industry for some time already, and explained this to the manager, together with practical market research examples she'd carried out before the meeting.

By contrast, when Caroline and Charly went to the bank to open the League of Her Own account, it was a completely different experience! Having been through the experience a couple of times each already, they were ready and prepared with a detailed business plan. The meeting went so well, then bank manager asked how he could sign his wife up to the service!

Accountancy

Whether you are registered as a sole trader or a Private Limited Company you will need to submit accounts to Companies House. From day one of your new business, set up a simple spreadsheet and make a note of any expenses, for example your first one might be registering for incorporation with Companies House, or registering your web address.

Every time you spend money on the business make a note of it. You will need it later and searching through your bank statements is no fun. Also don't forget to hold onto all receipts. They will be needed when you come to do your accounts.

If you are a registered company you will be given a date when your accounts are due and you must submit before this date. If you don't the company will be fined. If you are a sole trader you will be given a date your Self-Assessment is due, again you must submit by this date.

Both Charly and Caroline use qualified accountants, and believe us, it is worth every penny. If, however you are confident and comfortable in doing your own accounts by all means go ahead.

There are hundreds of different accountants, all charging different rates. Try websites like www.elance.com to find a reputable freelancer or check out the yellow pages for a local accountant.

"Get yourself a good accountant. When you're growing quickly it's absolutely key to be fully on top of the numbers so you can make the best decision possible. A good accountant will make sure they're available at the press of a button."

Pip Murray, Pip & Nut

Top Tip

You can get free online bookkeeping software to keep track of your accounts such as www.gnucash.org or www.turbocash.net If you require something with a bit more depth check out www.mybusinesworks.co.uk which will give you all the accounting tools you need.

Wrap Up

Setting up a business is no small task – and that's clear from the length of this chapter. But you shouldn't let that put you off. Take your time, and do everything step-by-step. Identify the things and the areas you can deal with yourself, and those where you need expert assistance. Don't be afraid to ask for help – you're not in this alone.

Section 5 - Attracting Clients

26. Power of speech

Get Talking

You'll be surprised how effective word of mouth can be. Once your business is up and running, talk about it! Get the word out there. Even if someone isn't in your target audience it's still worthwhile talking about what you do, as people are connected.

You never know who they know, how they may be able to help you and who they might pass on information to. Likewise, the more you talk about your company, the better your 'pitch' will become, so that when someone important asks you about it, you'll be well practiced speaking about the business.

Once you're up and running, we highly recommend putting yourself up for public speaking opportunities. Whether it's searching Twitter for journalists using the hashtag #journorequest for people to talk about a particular subject, or searching out public speaking engagements, get word out there! If you need some encouragement, we have a special module on 'Visibility' inside A League of Her Own.

"Perhaps the most surprising and most effective marketing tool we have discovered has been public speaking. Public speaking has allowed me to show who we truly are as a business whilst connecting and adding value to our ideal clients."

Lucy Chamberlain, C&C Search

27. Social Media

Social media is an incredible marketing tool. It's free and it can reach millions of people.

Social media has several advantages.
They allow you to:
• Engage with thousands of people from your local area and worldwide
• Increase the number of people visiting your website – so make sure you include your web address in your bio
• Generate a buzz about your business by letting people know what's going on
• Keep up-to-date on what's going on in your industry by following relevant people/businesses, including your competitors.
• Impress potential clients. Up-to-date social media accounts show you are serious, genuine, and active in your industry.
• Connect with competitors and fellow entrepreneurs all around the world.

Just be careful you don't sign up for too many social media accounts. Keeping an active social media account takes time, and if you're in business on your own, you're unlikely to be able to maintain more than 2 forms of social media well at any one time.

 Bear in mind that social media feeds need to be more than just business promotion. Otherwise people will lose interest.

To make your social media accounts work for you:

• Engage with others, and respond to their questions.
• Post interesting updates and advice, keep your posts varied
• Ask questions to get conversations going. If people make an effort to respond ensure you 'like, favourite or retweet'. Show you appreciate their comment.
• Use images in your posts - people like pictures and they stand out in social media.
• Pick your main pictures wisely. What do they say about you?
• Try to get a simple handle which matches your company / domain name and ideally use the same handle across different media platforms.

Remember that different forms of social media work for different things. Instagram and Twitter are great for building an audience. While Instagram is obviously a very visual form of social media, don't feel your business has to have lots of original photos to appear on Instagram. Quotes work really
well, and apps like Canva can help you create your own quotes and pictures very simply. Facebook can work well if you have an established audience. NB - if you decide you'd like to do Facebook or Instagram advertising, you will need a business Facebook account.

Top Tip

Managing lots of social media accounts can be time-consuming and confusing. Consider using a free tool such as Hootsuite to manage all your accounts in one place.

Tools will allow you to preschedule your posts. Just make sure you also check in on a daily basis, so you can respond in real time to any comments your followers make.

28. Advertising

Advertising is the most traditional way of promoting a business. There are endless opportunities to advertise including on Google, on blogs and websites, via social media, tv, newspapers, radio, magazine, billboards and directories such as the yellow pages.

The more traditional types of advertising such as newspapers and magazines can be very expensive so it's good to research other options first (including potentially getting PR in the papers or magazines instead of paying for advertising space).

Internet advertising

There are hundreds of websites you can advertise on, from high-end luxury magazines to well-read blogs. The costs vary hugely, and range from a few pounds to thousands. More commonly though, people use Google Adwords to advertise online.

Google Adwords is an online advertising program which enables your advert to appear on Google.

A simple way to see adverts using adwords is to type 'dating coach London' into Google. You will see the top 4 results have 'Ad' beside them. These are paid adverts. You will notice that as you have recently searched for dating coaches in London, relevant adverts will start appearing even if you are looking on a travel website for example. This is Google Adwords.

Adwords works on a keyword basis. You choose keywords (2 – 4 word phrases) which trigger you advert to appear. Google has to decide which advert should go at the top and unsurprisingly that space goes to the business which pays the most!

Adwords works in a similar way to an auction. You place your 'bid' (how much you're willing to pay maximum) for your ad to appear if someone searches your keyword. The top bid goes at the top of the search results. Depending on your chosen keywords, how popular they are and what other people have already bid will influence how much you have to pay for your advert to appear on the first page. It could be a couple of pence or several pounds. Some keywords Caroline uses cost approximately £6 per one click. That can soon add up so you may want to consider using cheaper but still relevant keywords. Obviously the cost of what you're selling will affect how much you're willing to pay per click.

There is lots of guidance available on Adwords and it's wise to have a good read and play around before going ahead. You can stop and start Adwords at any time and you can set a maximum payment, for example you will spend no more than £200 in total. You can find out more at https://accounts.google.com

Social media advertising

You may opt to advertise your products or services via social media such as Facebook. This allows you to promote your page to targeted individuals, for example you can target people based on sex, age, location.

Facebook will work out how much it will cost you to get a certain number of 'likes' (estimate) on your business Facebook page. You can stop and start your advertising campaign at any time and can set a daily maximum budget.

Top Tip

Make sure your Facebook ad looks the part. If it doesn't look appealing, nobody will click on it. If you need help check our websites such as www.fiverr.com or www.fivesquids.co.uk where you can have someone design your Facebook ad/page for a fiver, great value!

Magazines

Magazine advertising is often restricted to big brands, as it can be very expensive, especially the more well known the magazine. However magazine advertising may be a good option if your niche has a well-read local magazine in your target area.

Magazine advertising wasn't a success for Caroline and Mutual Attraction, but depending on your target audience and budget, it may be appropriate to advertise your services. Draw up a list of magazines and ask for their advertising pack. This should include key information about their readership, for example how many people read the magazine, their sex, age and average income. If this information is not provided be sure to ask for it as it will help you decide whether it is the right route for your business.

True Story

Caroline is a firm believer that you have to try everything once.

How do you know what's going to be best for your business and your clients unless you try something out? That's what led her to try print advertising. She took a small ad that cost the earth (the same cost as a small PR project) in the back of a luxury magazine for Londoners, which was given out free in the wealthier areas. She didn't get a single enquiry. Not one.

It was a hard pill to swallow. She had wasted a lot of money on something that bought her no benefits. Her experience in print advertising was a big downer and whilst it's not something she will be queuing up to do again anytime soon, don't rule it out completely.

Caroline's problem was that she jumped in the deep end when she should have tried out a small local paper first, where the costs are nowhere near as high. It also depends on your target audience. With all methods of advertising, you need to be constantly thinking 'would my target audience be reading this?'

Tracking what works for you

If you invest time and money in advertising you need to know whether it has worked. This is where Google Analytics comes in.

Google Analytics is a free service that generates detailed statistics about a website's traffic including where visitors come from, what they do on the site and which keywords bring people to the website.

Helpful information analytics can tell you:

● How many people visited your website - you can select a month, day, or timeframe
● How many visitors were unique and how many had visited before
● Where visitors came from, for example which country and city
● Visitors' age group and sex
● What pages visitors looked at and how long they spent on each page
● Which words and phrases people used which led to your website appearing in the Google search

Most importantly for advertising, Google Analytics will tell you exactly what people clicked on to get to your website – for example a Twitter link, a blog post, a directory listing and so on. This is very important and you may be surprised to find that not everything you think will work does.

For example Caroline wrote one particular blog post in particular that brings in more people than every other blog post she's written combined.

The findings from Google Analytics will shape how you advertise and attract clients and it's a completely free tool, - bonus!

For more information visit
www.google.com/intl/en_uk/analytics/

29. Business Cards

There's no point networking and not having a card with your details on for your new friend. Everyone loves a good business card, and if you're practicing talking more about your new business, then it's a great way to finish the conversation, and stay on someone's radar!

Obviously your chosen area of business will determine how much networking you do. Both of us run service-based companies, and we find business cards indispensable. We always have a couple in our handbags and wallets. Remember – business cards aren't just for potential clients. The reality of networking is that you meet tons of people who may be helpful to your business in some way.

It's not a necessity to spend a fortune on your business cards. There are plenty of places online you can get quality business cards done at an affordable price.

> www.vistaprint.co.uk
> www.moo.com

Business Tip

"Build a broad network. They will support you in what you're doing now and what you want to do in 10 years time. Luckily, this has been an occupational hazard with TableCrowd."

Kate Jackson, TableCrowd

30. Media Appearances

Media appearances can be an incredible way to gain credibility and free publicity. Depending on which industry you choose to work in, there are a whole variety of opportunities – from contributing a single quote for a magazine or newspaper article, to writing an entire article, to radio and TV appearances.

Ideally, establish yourself as an expert in your area of business. This may take some time, and require you to write a blog, self-publish a book or record a regular podcast. If you can establish yourself as a leading voice on a topic which may appear on TV or in the press, then you may benefit from free PR in the form of these appearances.

Remember, you're unlikely to be the only expert on a topic keen to share their expertise, because everyone has something they are trying to sell!

There are various ways to stand out and improve your chances of getting such appearances

• Be easily contactable – make sure journalists can find your email and check it regularly
• Regularly check and update your social media
• Get involved with topical conversations
• Be flexible – appearances may come at short notice and awkward times of day
• Live close to major cities – you will need to get to radio or TV stations easily

Personal branding is a big part of business these days – it ties into PR and your brand story, and can be a great way to get word out about your services or products. If you'd like more help with Personal Branding, do check out our module on the subject inside A League of Her Own.

31. Blogging

You can either have a blog on your business webpage or your own blog. If you're a keen blogger why not have both?!

Business blogging

Blogging can be a great way to make people aware of your services or products. Whilst blogging may not directly bring clients to your door (your readers may be from across the globe) it will help make your website more searchable if you write your posts with niched key words.

In its simplest terms the more people you have visiting and looking around your webpage the more important Google thinks your website is. Write your blog posts using key words and people may find your website from searching that term.

Personal blogging

Depending on your area of business, a personal blog could be really useful. We both use personal blogs a bit like online CVs, and these have really helped us both to establish ourselves as experts, and make it very easy for journalists to get in touch with us.

Use sites such as www.wordpress.com or www.blogger.com and you can set up your own blog using a simple template then get writing. This can be a great way to raise your professional profile.

http://www.carolinebrealey.co.uk/

Charly established herself as an industry expert, and someone who cared immensely about the dating industry, thanks to her personal blog '30 Dates'. While she never directly monetised the blog, it allowed her to establish opinions on key topics affecting singles, and polish her dating advice as the blog developed. https://30datesblog.com/ It even acted as a 'character reference' when she approached the online dating trade body to support her idea for the Dating Awards in the company's early stages.

Charly also has a 'CV' like blog which showcases her 'best bits'. She updates this regularly and it is through this site that most journalists contact her for media work – https://charlylester.com/

Some key pointers

- Keep your posts short – aim for 350 to 500 words. People have short attention spans!
- Use images – they capture attention
- Just make sure you have permission to use them and they aren't too large. If they take too long to download, people will go elsewhere for the information.
- Swat up on 'keywords' – SEO is your friend. You need to be writing about the subjects people want to read about!
- Make sure your blog template is 'mobile responsive' – it looks good on whatever device someone accesses it on. Check it out on your phone, laptop and an iPad.
- Be consistent – post regularly and try to keep a consistent voice. If you have multiple writers, make it clear who is writing.
- Make posts easy to share by adding sharing buttons – just don't add more than 4.

For more help with blogging, check out our bespoke module inside the League.

Top Tip

Be realistic about your time, because blogging is time-consuming. Whilst Caroline blogs regularly on her personal blog, she commits to writing twice per month for Mutual Attraction with the aim of getting it to once a week.

If you struggle to write, make the most of days when you are feeling inspired to write a couple of posts and then save them and post them on a regular basis. This way you don't have to force yourself to write once a week, or when you're not feeling so inspired.

Be professional in your blog, don't discuss clients and remember that whatever you put may be read by current or potential clients.

32. Public Relations (PR)

You may think of PR as something only large companies invest in, but even as you launch your business, your survival and success will depend on your reputation. Every day we are influenced by what we read, see and hear. If a friend tells us the food at a restaurant they visited was fabulous we are likely to consider going there. If you read about the bad practices of your favourite coffee shop, you may be more inclined to get your caffeine fix elsewhere. We all have opinions which we share with one another and these perceptions and opinions drive our decision as to whether or not we will use a service or buy a product. This is why your reputation as a business is absolutely critical.

When starting out, good referrals can be hard to achieve. You need a good reputation to bring in clients, but without clients in the first place how can you be expected to gain a good reputation?! It's a vicious circle, but one you can break with effective PR. This will manage your reputation and tell your story to the public on your behalf. The other main advantage for a start-up is that good PR can spread the word that you exist! This is one of the main challenges that any business faces.

You have two options when it comes to PR – enlist a professional or do it yourself (which isn't as hard as you might think).

PR Company

A PR company will positively promote your business by getting editorial coverage. This may include your story appearing on websites, in a magazine, the newspapers or on TV. A good PR company will be well-connected, creative and be able to write exciting stories on your behalf to write in a press release which will then be distributed to all their contacts.

A press release outlines a story or information that will be beneficial for the public to read. Newspapers and reporters pick out the most interesting and relevant stories to publish or use in their work.

Writing an engaging press release can be a challenge but a PR company will be experienced in writing them well.

The downside of using a PR company is that they can be expensive. Expect to pay a starting fee of around £2,000 for a small project. If this is out of your budget try sourcing a freelancer who will have more control over their price structure.

True Story

Caroline enlisted the support of a PR company to help her launch Mutual Attraction. It was the best thing she could have done.

Interviews with her started cropping up on different websites and she was called to give quotes and examples for articles in the press. The big turnaround came when she got a one-page spread in both Glamour magazine and the Sunday People newspaper. Both included a cheesy romantic photo and focussed on different aspects of matchmaking; one about her becoming a matchmaker and the other focussed on dating advice. Both were successful and she soon had a steady stream of clients at her door and Mutual Attraction officially took off.

Obviously it's worth bearing in mind that Caroline's matchmaker business is very magazine-friendly, and at the time she started her company, there weren't many matchmakers around, particularly younger ones, targeted at Caroline's demographic.

DIY PR

If you haven't got the budget for a PR professional you can always give it a go yourself. Both Charly and Caroline have had a great deal of success doing their own PR - get creative and you can get good coverage with little or no budget.

Write your own Press Release

Got a story worth telling? Write your own press release and submit to a news distribution site for a small fee. Journalists register with news distribution sites as a way of getting access to all the up to date news and they will be able to read your press release, which may get picked up for print/tv/radio or any other media outlet. You will be able to see who has used your press release so you can track progress.

www.sourcewire.com offers a press release distribution service from just £50. Caroline has submitted press releases via this channel and several had a great response, one in particular about being nominated for an Award.

The key to getting more exposure is to write a good story -

Here are few tips to get you started:

- Make sure you're targeting the right journalists. Don't just send out your press release to anyone and everyone. Personalise the emails. Often we send a taster email to the journalists before sending over the press release once their interest is piqued.
- Make it interesting. Think carefully about why this is a story which the journalist needs to be telling.
- If you're writing a press release, keep it no longer than one page. Journalists are busy people and receive hundreds of press releases each week.
- Photos can really help, but make sure they aren't huge. You can always send over higher resolution versions if the journalists require high quality ones for printing.
- Don't make it promotional, it will be discarded instantly.
- Provide details on where the reader can find out more information e.g. link to your website and ensure your contact details are clearly highlighted, make it easy for them to contact you.

Top Tip

Haven't got an exciting story to tell at the moment? Why not do your own poll or survey on a topic related to your area of business?

Caroline conducted a poll on kissing and her findings were published in a range of magazines –

http://www.cosmopolitan.co.uk/love-sex/dating-guide/dating-research-reveals-the-ultimate-kissing-turn-off

For more advice on doing your own PR, check out our PR module in 'A League of Her Own'. We have created a 3 hour-long module on the topic!

Micro PR

Micro PR relates to the day-to-day interactions you will have with the public. Every interaction should be positive. Is every email enquiry responded to promptly? Is every phone caller greeted with a genuinely cheery tone? Do people feel positive after speaking with you?

Section 6 – Making Sales

33. Your 'Shop Front'

These days, for most of us, our 'shop front' is our website. It's our first point of contact with our customers, and for some people, it's the only point of contact. So, as we mentioned in the previous section, it's important to have a website you're proud of, and to regularly update it.

But your 'shop front' extends elsewhere across your business. It is reflected in your social media, your mail outs, and the way you present your business at networking events.

You may decide to have actual premises – either a shop or office, depending on your area of business - however it is worth bearing in mind how much of an initial expense this will be. Rent really isn't cheap, so think carefully about whether you need a physical space for your business, or if you can exist online. If you are offering a service, it can be easier (and cheaper) to work remotely, and either meet clients at their offices, or if you are 'B2C' (Business-to-Customer) then you could consider meeting them in public places instead.

Neither Caroline nor Charly have offices, despite running profitable 6 figure businesses.

Members' Club

If you are in a big city consider buying membership to a private members club. Every club operates differently but they will all charge a membership fee ranging from a few hundred to several thousand pounds. Membership will enable you to access the amenities which usually include a bar and lounge area, restaurant and meeting rooms. They normally have an exclusive feel about them and without membership you are unlikely to be allowed entrance. A members club is a great place to hold an initial consultation and it is worth considering investing in membership if you do not go down the traditional office route.

The other main advantage is that it can double up for an office as previously mentioned, whilst you probably wouldn't be able to base yourself there 9-5 every day you could certainly work there for part of the week.

True Story

Just make sure you choose the club wisely. Charly once joined a private members' club, which proved a complete waste of money – overpriced, small and not open at the times of day she needed to have meetings.

Hotel

A beautiful hotel bar and lounge area is Caroline's ideal location to hold an initial consultation for her matchmaking agency. Why? It's free, has good service, reasonable prices, accessible, has Wi-Fi and with people coming and going you will not draw attention to yourself or potential client.

Pick your hotel wisely - Caroline has several which she uses regularly and she uses them because they tick all the above boxes as well as being very close to a tube station for convenience.

Whilst your local 2* hotel may not quite have the charm or set the tone for the meeting, a good hotel can provide the perfect environment for an initial consultation. This is a great venue choice when starting out.

Home

There are a number of service providers who hold initial consultations in either their own home or the client's home. Meeting someone in their own home can allow you to gain a clearer picture of the person as a whole. However you should always be wary of doing this. If you do go down this route, and decide to meet a client in their own home, please ensure you leave full contact details of where you are with others and never go unaccompanied.

Personally neither of us would opt to meet people in their home unless absolutely necessary, for safety reasons. While we both have home-offices, we never have meetings at home. We also appreciate our privacy and don't conduct business in our own homes, however depending on your location, set-up and comfort, you may choose to conduct meetings at home.

On a separate note – if you use a home office for your day-to-day business (regardless of whether you do meetings in your home), a portion of your rent or mortgage fees, council tax, electricity, phone bill and broadband will be tax deductible.

34. First Impressions

In the same way you will be forming an opinion on your potential client, they will be putting together one of you!

Giving the right impression is critical and if you get it wrong can lose you a sale.

Packaging

These days, a large number of shops only exist online. While this means you don't need a physical shop space, you will still need to factor in storage.

It's also important to consider what your goods look like when you send them out to customers. We live in a world of Instagram, and a great way to get free publicity for your brand is if someone takes a photo of their purchase and shares it on their social media. A way to increase the likelihood of that happening is to think carefully about how you send out your goods. Small businesses are getting very good at sending out personalised thank you cards and cheap freebies – like stickers or branded postcards – with their products.

Meeting Up

If you're meeting a client in person, here are a few tips which can help with making a good first impression.

● Be there first, get yourself settled and relaxed. You want to appear calm and collected. Racing in at the last minute looking frazzled won't be the best start!

● Reserve ahead. Some of the hotel bars where Caroline meets clients can get very busy so she always ensures she reserves a table beforehand.

● Look the part by being well groomed and dressing professionally.

● Have everything you need at your fingertips including any forms, pens and business cards.

● Keep your work phone at the ready. If someone is running late or lost they will need to get hold of you. Caroline has noticed that women in particular like to call her when they are walking into the hotel so they are able to easily recognise her.

● To assist with recognition, Caroline shares her LinkedIn profile with people when confirming a consultation so they can clearly see her photo and recognise her. People feel more comfortable and confident knowing who they are meeting.

• Welcome the person warmly with a genuine smile and make it your task to make them feel comfortable. Initially make general chit-chat, ask them if they found the venue ok and if they would like a drink.

• Focus on the positives but be honest, little white lies might seem harmless but are likely to be found out down the line.

• If you are asked a question and you're not sure of the answer, tell them you will find out and get back to them, you're only human and initially clients can throw up things you aren't sure about, it's all part of the process!

• At the end of the meeting thank them for their time.

• Follow up in an email after the meeting answering any final questions. Make sure you do this as soon as possible; if they need your services, they won't want to hang around!

As long as you are positive, honest, and answer their questions they will leave happy and hopefully ready to sign up for your services!

35. Selling Your Service

The big sell! If you come from a sales background then you have a real advantage here but if not there's no need to panic because you can teach yourself to be a great seller. (This section will be of most relevance if you are selling a high ticket service).

Can you answer yes to this question?

'Do I believe in the service I'm selling?'

If yes then you are halfway there. Really believing in what you are selling will make you more natural in your technique and your passion for what you do will shine through.

Pain points

Almost every product or service is designed to solve a problem. Sometimes it's just a bit more complicated to work out what problem you are solving. What is your client's 'pain point'? What is the problem you are able to solve for them. The more aware you are of the pain point, the better your sell will be, because you can solve their problems before they even raise them.

Some proven techniques are all you need to get going:

Have an agenda

Write down the key areas you need to cover in the meeting. If the conversation keeps deviating then bring them back to the key points you need to discuss.

By all means let your client talk freely but you should be guiding the conversation.

Make a mental note of what you want to achieve from the meeting.
Points you may have on your agenda:

- Introduce yourself and the service
- Learn about the person
- Discuss what client can expect
- Outline your various packages, if relevant
- Service fees
- Testimonials
- Do they have any questions?

Focus on them not you

Don't get carried away talking about yourself, it's easy done especially if you're feeling a tad nervous. Relate what you're talking about to them by using the terms 'you' and 'your' instead of 'I' and 'me'.

Highlight the benefits

How will they benefit from your service? How will their lives be better because they are using it? Outline all the advantages of using your service.

Listen

Listen to what they have to say. If they feel comfortable they will open up to you. Let them explain the problems they are facing. Where possible this will allow you to tailor your service to their needs. Ask intuitive questions which show you are listening and that you understand their circumstances.

Don't hard sell

Nobody likes a hard sell and if you are offering a personal service, you will need to build a rapport with your customer. Give people the time and space to decide whether it's right for them.

Your selling technique will get better with practice and experience, and as you become more confident.

Getting to know them

If you are offering a high-end service, it can be useful to offer a free, initial consultation.

The reasons for this are

1) To give them the information they need to make an informed decision whether your service is right for them.
2) To get to know them.
3) To work out if they are right for your service. Remember, the consultation is two-way.
4) To begin building a rapport.

If you want to take notes, let the person know beforehand and by all means have an agenda in front of you but try to avoid simply asking the questions in a way you would at an interview.

If you have a form or questionnaire you'd like your prospective client to complete, we suggest you allow them to do so in the comfort of their own home. This gives them the chance to think over their answers instead of putting them on the spot.

Top Tip

If you like to take notes during meetings, consider investing in an iPad or tablet with a pen.

You can then design your own form for free at websites such as http://jotformeu.com and make your notes directly onto the form using the questions to guide the conversation. You can share your notes with the person and if there's anything you need them to sign they can do it there and then. Much more professional than having lots of paper floating around and you'll look the part to! Alternatively a voice recorder is a smart alternative to making sure you don't miss or forget any important information. Just remember to ask before you record anything.

"Celebrate the small successes. In fact someone told me but it took some time for me to understand what he meant by that."

Stephanie Eltz, Doctorify

36. Contracts

The initial consultation went well and the person wants to use your services. Whilst you might be chomping at the bit to get going, you need to ensure all appropriate paperwork is completed.

A Contract

A contract is a legally binding agreement that outlines both parties' responsibilities. We strongly recommend that you have a contract professionally drawn up - it is worth the investment.

If you have not trained in law then writing a contract from scratch is hugely challenging. The contract is an important legal document and throwing together one with no experience is likely to result in a contract with loop-holes and errors. Your contract needs to be watertight, both for your clients' benefit and yours.

You can buy contracts 'off the shelf' and edit them to fit your service. However you may find this too restrictive, and not a good fit for the packages, which you offer. However it can still give you the back bone of the contract and you can flesh it out yourself.
See www.business-in-a-box.com for examples.

If you are signing a contract drawn up by someone else – for example if you are working Business to Business and your client asks you to sign a contract – make sure to read it carefully. We recommend seeking legal advice where possible so you are fully up to speed with the small print.

Solicitors

Check out the Yellow Pages and draw up a list of solicitors in your area. Give them a call and ask for a quote. Alternatively use the freelancer route again. Caroline's original contract was drawn up by a qualified solicitor who was advertising his services through www.peopleperhour.com, and under £100 later she had a professional contract.

Before you go down this route make sure you have figured out all the ins and outs of what needs to be covered as the solicitor may not know the specific information that needs to be present for your field of expertise.

To guide you, consider using the following sub headings:

Introduction

Here you should include your business name, registered number and registered address. Define any key words you will be using throughout the agreement.

What you are offering

This part needs to go into detail on the service you are offering.

What exactly is included in the package he or she is purchasing?

For example how many sessions will be included? What constitutes a session? When will your services come to an end? It's important to define any terms you use. What happens if the client fails to attend a session, or is late to a session? What happens if you are required to cancel a session, or arrive late to a session?

Fees

How much are you charging for your services and when is payment due? Don't forget to include how the client must pay you and include any bank details. What happens if they don't pay on time? If there is an option to pay in installments, how much is each installment? Make it clear and transparent for the client so they know exactly how much they are paying.

If you are invoicing a business, make sure you are aware of their invoicing procedure. Some businesses require a Purchase Order number. Others may take up to 28 days to pay you, so you may prefer to invoice at the start of your services, to ensure you are paid in a timely manner.

"Don't be afraid to ask to be paid more or to pay someone less. I'm terrible at asking for money and haggling and have definitely been screwed over in the past."

Hannah Witton, YouTuber & Author

Top Tip

Try to have as many options as possible available for clients to pay, for example via direct transfer, cheque and PayPal. Make it as easy as possible for clients to pay you.

Cancellation

Outline what your cancellation policy is. This is a good place to write about your 'cooling off period' and to outline what will happen if a client chooses to end the services and what happens if you can no longer provide services. For example if they cancel will they be entitled to a refund and if so how much?

Under what circumstances can you cancel the services and how much warning do you have to provide? If you cancel their course of sessions, will you refund any of their fee? If you are selling tickets, are they transferable or refundable? Make your terms clear.

Privacy

Privacy is likely to be very important to clients. Outline what clients can expect from you for example that you will not share their personal information and will protect and store their information safely. Ensure you are fully up to speed with the GDPR – General Data Protection Regulations – invoked in May 2018.

Confidentiality agreement

Depending on the nature of your work, you may choose to have a confidentiality agreement or statement. These can either be worked into your contract or you can have them as a stand-alone document. If you are offering a service to other businesses, they may have their own confidentiality agreement which they wish you to sign.

Whilst you will have already touched on privacy in the contract, a confidentiality statement will be appreciated by clients in certain areas – for instance matchmaking and personal coaching services. If you do adopt such a statement, make sure they know what they tell you will be in confidence and that their information will not be placed online.

Last but not least, make sure the contract is signed and dated by both parties. Once it's signed you're ready to roll!

Useful Resources

http://www.clickdocs.co.uk/ advertises a contract suitable for a dating agency for the cost of £22+Vat.

Business Contracts Kit For Dummies by Harroch, Richard D (2011) available on Amazon.

Section 7 – Staying on Track

"I fail every day and if I am not successful it's just not the end."

Stephanie Eltz, Doctorify

37. Customer Service

Looking after your clients and providing excellent customer service is essential if you are to make your clients experience a positive one. Aim to provide outstanding customer service to every one of your clients by following these guidelines.

Make clients feel important and appreciated

Always use their first name and treat them as an individual person and not just a number. It creates a good vibe and will make the partnership between you stronger. If you offer a high value service – like coaching – make a point of knowing what's going on in your client's life, for example if they have a new job send them a congratulations card. Little actions can go a long way.

Even if you only have brief encounters with clients – such as posting out your products – remember that these encounters matter and make each opportunity to resonate with your customer count!

Keep it professional

Depending on the nature of your business, you may get to know your clients very well over the course of time. Whilst it's nice that they know a little about you, remember they are a client and not a Facebook friend! Keep it professional (and don't accept friend requests!).

Get feedback

It's not just important to get feedback, you need to reflect and act on it. Perhaps you could conduct a questionnaire or poll or carry out short interviews with clients. Whichever method you choose, make sure you ask questions that will give you valuable insight into your client's experience and thoughts.

You will never be an objective client of your own service, so it's important to listen to what your clients do have to say. Try not to be defensive or offended by any comments they make. Everybody is entitled to her own opinion and dealing with their feedback professionally will show you genuinely appreciate their feedback.

Top Tip

If you make a change based on someone's feedback don't forget to let them know. This will empower your client, make them feel important and happy that you have listened to what they had to say.

Be available

Answer emails punctually – you should never leave an email more than 48 hours unless you are on holiday and have a clear 'Out of Office' set up. For some bespoke high-end services, it's important to be available by phone during working hours, so get a business phone number. Remember you can switch off a phone outside of work hours to ensure clients only contact you during reasonable hours.

Freebies

Everyone loves a freebie and your clients will be no exception. If you've written an ebook, why not give them a complimentary copy? Caroline regularly tries to find deals and offers for her clients, for example a complimentary ticket to a dating event. Get creative; there are so many opportunities out there.

A newsletter can be a great way to stay in touch with clients (and prospective clients) and to provide them with freebies! Just make sure they have actively opted in, so you comply with the recent GDPR changes. If you do send out a newsletter, keep people engaged with freebies and tasters of your services. Film videos, provide taster advice and show prospective clients how good you are at what you do.

Don't promise what you can't deliver

'Under promise, over deliver' is a saying for a reason - it works. Make promises you know you can keep and then aim to go above and beyond.

How to deal with a complaint:

Not everyone is happy 100% of the time. If a client complains ...

• Respond quickly. Whilst you don't need to offer a solution at this point, acknowledge your clients complaint and tell them you will look into it.
• Apologise that they are unhappy and that they have had to come to you with a complaint. You are not apologising for what's happened (this may not be your fault) but you are recognising that you don't want them to be unhappy.
• Make notes and keep a record of the complaint. Think it over before responding to the client - a quick reactive response may be the only option you can think of at the time but take some time to think it over.
• Be positive and try to take an optimistic approach to the complaint.
• Do all you can to make the client happy if it's in your power to do so.

- Recognise there are some things that will be out of your control.
- Try to respond in a human way – sometimes the easiest way to diffuse an angry person is to remind him or her that you are a real person, that you are trying your best, that mistakes happen etc.

Top Tip

Consider having a specific complaints policy which outlines how complains will be dealt with and sets out steps for what a complainant should expect to happen e.g. you will get back to then within 72 hours.

There will always be things that are out of your control.

If you have made a slip up and the complaint is valid, then gracefully admit to it and do all you can to fix it. However there will be times when it is out of your control and in these cases you need to be very clear with clients where your responsibilities start and finish. You cannot control the actions of others.

With Charly's Awards program, she set up a transparent complaint and review system – due to the nature of her business. She's never had to use it, but just knowing the procedure to review judges' decisions was in place gave her reassurance, and something she could tell disgruntled entrants or finalists.

"Making mistakes allows me to learn from them in order to make better informed decisions. And once those decisions are made and my goals are achieved, to me, that is success."

Michelle Hua, Made with Glove and Women of Wearables

38. Growing your Business

Once your business is up and running, your thoughts will move towards expansion. Maybe you haven't got world domination in your sights but you may want to grow the number of clients you're working with or add more aspects to your services. Your business will also need to evolve to reflect the changing world we live in. For example the demographics of your local area may change making it no longer viable to offer the niche you do. Other experts will crop up which will make you re-evaluate your own service and make changes.

Mutual Attraction has evolved hugely since Caroline launched, and Charly's services have changed immensely in the last four years. Her Awards spread from the UK to the US and Europe and grew from Awards to also running Conferences.

Caroline's business hasn't necessarily grown in the way she thought it would, but it has evolved and changed in response to new knowledge, her strengths and the changing world of dating and matchmaking in London.

Charly ended up working with a number of businesses on PR projects, after they realised that she was doing her own PR for The Dating Awards and getting better coverage than PR companies were for them.

You shouldn't be afraid of trying new things with your business - far from it! You won't know what's right for you, your business and your clients until you try it. The key is to be switched on with what's going on around you. We read local and national blogs. We have Google Alerts set up for industry news. We stay in regular contact with our industry network, and Caroline regularly checks competitor websites and listens to what people are telling her. Especially potential clients who decide not to join Mutual Attraction. The reason why may not be what you think.

Here are a few suggestions to keep you and your business on the right track.

Continue to Skill-Up

No matter how experienced you are, adding skills and knowledge to your offering will only help. Charly is a massive fan of masterclasses, and tries to attend at least a few events each month. Online learning can also be a great way to learn new skills at your own pace.

Find a Mentor

As we've already mentioned, mentoring is a professional relationship where an experienced person (the mentor) assists and supports another (the mentored/mentee) in developing knowledge and skills to improve their personal and business development. For example a mentor could be an experienced expert directly from your industry or someone who has achieved a great deal in another field, which could directly relate to your business, such as Marketing.

A mentor's role is to provide a sounding board, to offer constructive feedback, to challenge you to move beyond your comfort zone, to encourage growth by shared learning and networks and to support you in achieving your goals.

Whilst some mentors charge for this service there are plenty of not for profit organisations that offer a mentoring service for free. Charly is a mentor at her old university and a number of universities offer similar programmes. Alternatively, why not reach out to someone who inspires you and ask them whether they would consider being your mentor.

Think of people in your extended network, family friends and even your competition. Thanks to technology your mentor could be anywhere in the world. Mentoring could be an hour a week, a monthly session or can be more intense. There are no set rules and this can be decided between yourself and your mentor.

"The best piece of business advice I've been given is the importance of having a mentor, I've always looked for advice and guidance for people who are where I want to be, even if that has involved literally 'buying' their friendship through paying to join their organisations or have them as a personal mentor. It is well worth the money!"

Natasha Courtenay-Smith, Digital Strategy & PR Expert

True Story

Did you know that Christian Dior was Yves St Laurent's mentor? Other famous mentors include Usher who spotted a potential new star when he watched YouTube videos of a young Justin Bieber!

Review your business plan and targets

Remember that business plan and those targets you set way back when?! Go back to them, review them and renew them. Every year we both set ourselves new targets for what we want to achieve in the next year – both personally and in business.

Examples of some of our targets include:
1) Increase revenue by 15%
2) Write this book
3) Launch an online training programme for female entrepreneurs
4) Take our businesses overseas

You will likely find that your targets will come to you quite naturally; the challenging part is outlining how you are going to achieve them!

Break down the target into smaller chunks of the different ways you will achieve the target and set deadlines (and stick to them!). This will keep you on track and keep you motivated.

"You have to put the business first at all times. You might have employees that you adore but if they are not a fit anymore then you have to recognize that. You are responsible for the wellbeing of the whole."

Stephanie Eltz, Doctorify

Keep ahead of the game

Keep researching, keep up to date on what your competition is doing and keep striving to improve your business. Even when you're at the top of the game raise your bar!

New Ventures

Consider expanding your service. Perhaps through your experience you've recognised a niche area that's not being catered for or perhaps you want to train up to offer additional services to your existing clients. There are opportunities everywhere, be open to new ideas.

True Story

Most of the exciting twists and turns in Charly's career have been reactive ones, rather than proactive ones. The Guardian approached her directly because of a blog post she wrote, and offered her a job. Don't be too fixed with your plans for the future – by being a bit flexible and being receptive to external offers, you may find the journey is a lot more exciting than even you imagined!

Partnership work

Working in partnership with other industry professionals can help grow your business ten-fold.

Obviously Caroline and Charly work closely together – and this is a partnership which has developed over the last few years. Caroline is Head Judge for Charly's international Awards, and Charly assists with the Matchmaker Academy training, specializing in the blogging and social media aspects of training.

Remember, it's very important that you only partner with people who have respected brands themselves. Otherwise you can risk damaging your reputation. It's definitely a case of quality over quantity.

"I don't really believe in mistakes, I believe in moving fast, breaking things, and learning fast. Some people break more things than others, but hopefully they are moving faster and learning more because of it."

Amanda Bradford, The League

39. Keeping Motivated

As you'll have seen from many of the quotes from the female founders in the book, we all have doubts at times. We're all human! And there will be ups and downs through out your business career! So how can you stay motivated?

Surround yourself with the right people

You need a good support group around you. Not everyone may understand what you're doing, but surround yourself with people who are positive and supportive. Sometimes you need to be selfish with your time and that includes not wasting it on people who will bring you down and make you worry even more.

Monthly notebooks

One of the ways Charly stays on track is by buying 12 lovely notebooks each year, and starting a new one every month. She records all her notes for that month in the book, and also starts it with a list of targets for all areas of her life. As she achieves them she checks them off, and if she doesn't get round to something, she carries it over to the following month's notebook. It's not only a good way to stay organized and motivated, but it allows her to look back over the year and appreciate everything she's achieved.

Set yourself the right challenges

With any challenges you set yourself, try to phrase them in such a way that you can't fail them if you have an off day. Charly often sets herself self-growth challenges – reading 52 books, or completing 300 days of exercise in a year. While they might not seem relevant to business, they are in two ways. Firstly, it's important to have a well-rounded life. You can't spend every waking hour working on your business, so setting time to read books, or go to the gym, will allow you to strike a work-life balance. Secondly, the way Charly sets her challenges, she can have a bad week or two and still stay on track. By setting herself a total for the entire year, rather than saying she needs to read a book every single week, or do 5 days exercise every week, it means that if she does have a bad week, she hasn't failed for the entire year.

Find an accountability partner

If you don't have a co-founder, then a peer mentor can work well as an 'accountability partner'. This is someone who you check in with on a regular basis to make sure you're staying on track, and remaining disciplined. The reality of working for yourself is that sometimes you will have ups and downs, and when things are going a bit badly, the worst thing you can do is give up and bury your head in the sand. By scheduling regular check-ups with an accountability partner, you can minimize the opportunity to trip yourself up and go off track.

Focus on you

It's easier said than done, but try not to compare yourself too much to your competitors. Particularly when things aren't going so well. Focus your energy on you and your business. In reality you never know how well someone else is doing – there can be a lot of smoke and mirrors in business.

When you go into business for yourself, your life is also likely to be very different to your friends' lives. So try not to compare your successes to those of your friends in full time roles.

Celebrate the wins

We've said it before, we'll say it again. Be your own biggest cheerleader.
When you hit a milestone, no matter how small, celebrate it! One of our friends sets 'Champagne Milestones' with his business partner. Every time they hit a set goal – whether it's a total number of sales, launching a new product, getting a good piece of PR or even launching a whole new company, they pop open a bottle of bubbly! We took his advice and popped open our own bottle of champagne the day we launched A League of Her Own.

Keep a record of all your company achievements. And next time your motivation is ebbing, or you are having a bit of a bad day, look at everything you've achieved!

40. Final Word

Congratulations, you've made it to the end of the book! In these 7 sections, we've covered all the areas of business which we believe are most useful and important when you are starting out alone.

We hope we've given you practical, useable advice, and that we've inspired you to join the ever-growing numbers of female business owners!

Good luck with your business, and do let us know if we can be of any more help. If you'd like the support of a network of peers and incredible role models, do come and check out A League of Her Own.

Running your own business truly is an adventure, and it can be a lot more enjoyable when you have others around you to share the ups and the downs. The League is packed full of lengthy modules on everything from Branding, to Social Media, Blogging, Public Speaking, Running Events, Getting Investment, to Podcasting and designing Online Courses. So if there is something in this book which you'd like some more help with, do come and take a look. Each month we cover a different area of business learning, in a one-hour tutorial video, and three expert interviews. We have workbooks, FAQ sheets, weekly challenges in the Facebook group, and live Q&A sessions. And if you live in the UK, we also run regular meet-up events for members.

As an extra incentive, we'd like to give you a special discount. Use the code BOOK30 for a £5 discount off our monthly subscription.

We look forward to meeting you in the League, and do please reach out to us over email or social media to let us know what you think of this book!

Charly and Caroline xx

Charly@leagueofher.com
@leagueofcharly
Caroline@leagueofher.com
@leagueofcarolin

26523404R00096

Printed in Poland
by Amazon Fulfillment
Poland Sp. z o.o., Wrocław